PICKLEBALL

FOR BEGINNERS

A Step-by-Step Guide to
Learning and Playing Pickleball

ETHAN JOHNSON

Table of Contents

Introduction

Explanation of pickleball

The paddle sport known as pickleball incorporates aspects of tennis, badminton, and ping pong into its gameplay. Everyone of any age or degree of expertise may have a good time playing this game because it is both entertaining and exciting.

Joel Pritchard, a congressman from Washington State, and Bill Bell, a businessman, are credited with inventing the sport of pickleball in the year 1965. The Pritchard family came up with the idea for the game first as a way to pass the time together during the warm summer months. The original pickleball court was laid out on asphalt in Pritchard's backyard, and it was there that the game was invented.

The history of the name "pickleball" is quite fascinating. The story goes that Pritchard's dog, Pickles, who would chase after the ball and bury it in the bushes, inspired the naming of the game. Pritchard, on the other hand, denied the rumor and stated that the name of the game was simply derived from a combination of the names of various sports.

Pickleball's popularity expanded over the years, and the game eventually made its way to other regions of the country. In 1976, the first pickleball tournament was played, and in 1984, the United States of America Pickleball Association was established. Pickleball is a popular sport that is practiced not only in the United States but also in the majority of other countries across the world.

You will require a few essential pieces of gear in order to play pickleball. The pickleball paddle, which has a form comparable to that of a table tennis paddle but is somewhat larger, is the most essential component of the game. The paddle is constructed out of a number of materials, the most notable of which are graphite, composite materials, and wood.

Pickleball is played with a ball that is comparable in size to a wiffle ball but has holes that are much smaller. Because it is not too heavy and can be hit with relative ease, the ball is ideal for players who are just starting out. Pickleball is played on a court that is of a rectangular shape and has a net in the middle to create two halves. The dimensions of the court for doubles play are 20 feet wide by 44 feet long, and the dimensions for singles play are 20 feet wide by 22 feet long.

The rules of pickleball are not too complicated and can be grasped with little effort. The first step of the game is the serve, which must be executed underhand and in a direction that is diagonal across the court. The team that is receiving the serve must wait for the ball to bounce before returning it, and the serve must land within the service court of the opposing team.

Following the delivery of the serve, the two teams may take turns hitting the ball back and forth across the net. Before a volley can be attempted, the ball must first be allowed to bounce once on either side of the net. When a ball touches the line, it is considered to have "in" status. When one team fails to return the ball to the other or hits it out of bounds, the other team scores a point.

The game of pickleball is normally played to 11 points, and the team that comes victorious must do so by a margin of at least two points. If the score is tied at 10-10, the winning team needs to win by a margin of at least two points in order to claim victory in the game. The terms "love," "15," "30," and "40" are used to indicate the score in pickleball. This scoring system is quite similar to that of tennis.

Pickleball is a sport in which one must become excellent in a number of fundamental techniques in order to play the game successfully. The first component is the grip, which has characteristics that are similar to those of the grip used in tennis. The player should hold the paddle with a grip that is firm but not tense, wrapping their fingers around the handle of the paddle.

The following technique that is extremely significant is footwork. When playing pickleball, it is essential to have a light, rapid step and have the ability to change directions quickly at any time. The player should maintain a ready position at all times, with their knees bent slightly and their weight distributed evenly over the balls of their feet.

A dink is a pickleball shot which is composed of a soft shot that gets hit just above the net. It is one of the most common shots in the game. This shot is often used to build up a volley or to force the opposing side to make a weak return. It can also be utilized to gain an advantage over the opponent. In order to successfully complete a dink, the player must keep their paddle low and in front of their body, and then hit the ball with a light flick of the wrist.

The volley is another key shot in the sport of pickleball. This shot is used when the ball hits in the air, and it entails hitting the ball before it bounces. A player must maintain their position with their paddle in front of their body and make contact with the ball at the highest point possible in order to successfully complete a volley.

Last but not least, the overhead smash is a powerful shot that can be utilized to put an end to a rally. When the ball is hit high in the air, this shot is executed by drawing the paddle back behind the body and then swinging it forward with force to knock the ball downwards.

It is necessary to have a strong strategy and tactical approach on playing pickleball, in addition to learning the basic techniques that are required to play the game. Playing a "soft game," in which the emphasis is placed on making consistent shots and causing the opposition team to make mistakes, is a common technique that is used in pickleball.

Playing a more aggressive game, with the primary goals to hit powerful shots and put pressure on the opposition side, is another technique that can be utilized. This strategy might be useful if the player in concern possesses a powerful overhead smash or is capable of hitting spin shots that are difficult to return.

It is essential to have an organized game plan and to be able to communicate clearly and efficiently with your doubles partner when playing doubles. The strategy of having one player play at the net while the other player plays at the baseline is one that is utilized frequently. This not only enables a good balance of offense and defense, but it also has the potential to throw off the other team's balance.

Even though pickleball is not as physically taxing as some other sports, it is still essential to maintain a healthy fitness level and practice in the correct manner if you want to give your best performance. Strength training can help enhance power and endurance, while flexibility and injury prevention workouts like warming up and stretching can help improve your range of motion and prevent injuries.

It is also essential to practice on a consistent basis and concentrate on getting better at specific aspects of your game. It's possible that this will require you to focus on your footwork, improve your accuracy and consistency, or come up with new strokes and approaches.

Pickleball is a very social sport, and there are many possibilities to connect with other players and to participate in local events and tournaments. This is one of the many reasons why pickleball is so enjoyable. The United States of America Pickleball Association is an excellent resource that can help you locate local pickleball courts and clubs, as well as provide additional information on the sport and put you in touch with other players.

You can also improve your skills and increase your understanding of the game by reading books, visiting websites, or watching instructional videos, all of which are readily available. You may quickly develop your skills and your passion for the game of pickleball if you make use of the resources that are available and get involved in the pickleball community.

In conclusion, pickleball is a sport that combines elements of tennis, badminton, and ping-pong, making it an enjoyable and interesting activity. In the world of pickleball, there is always something new to learn and explore, so it doesn't matter if you are just starting out or if you are a seasoned player. You can become a skilled and enthusiastic pickleball player by being proficient in the game's fundamental techniques, establishing solid methods and techniques, maintaining a healthy body and keeping connected to the community.

Brief history of pickleball

Pickleball is a sport that is actually not that old but has seen a surge in popularity in recent years. Joel Pritchard, who was a congressman from Washington State, and Bill Bell, who was a businessman, were the ones who came up with the idea in 1965. The Pritchard family came up with the game so that they would have something to do together during the warm summer months.

The game was first played on a badminton court with a net that had been lowered to a height of 36 inches when it was first invented. Ping-pong paddles and a perforated plastic ball that was about the same size as a wiffle ball were the equipment that the players utilized. The name "pickleball" was inspired by the dog that belonged to the Pritchard family and was once known as Pickles. The game was formerly known as "paddle tennis."

Pickleball's popularity expanded over the years, and the game eventually made its way to other regions of the country. The first ever pickleball club was founded in the city of Seattle in the 1970s, and the first ever pickleball tournament was played in Tukwila, Washington, in the same year. The popularity of the game continued to rise during the 1980s and 1990s, and in 1984, the USA Pickleball Association was established in response to the growing demand.

Pickleball has shown a meteoric rise in popularity over the past several years, particularly among people of retirement age. According to the Sports and Fitness Industry Association, participation in the sport of pickleball increased by 21.3% between the years 2016 and 2017, making it one of the sports with the fastest growth rate in the United States.

Origins of Pickleball

Pickleball may be traced back to the summer of 1965, when a congressman from Washington State named Joel Pritchard traveled to Bainbridge Island to spend time with his friend Bill Bell. This is when pickleball was first played. The family of Pritchard was seeking for something to do to pass the time, so they decided to build a badminton court in the backyard.

However, they quickly realized that they were missing some of the equipment, including the shuttlecock, which was a major setback. They were not disappointed by this setback, so they devised a plan B and substituted a ball made of perforated plastic. In addition to this, they dropped the height of the net to 36 inches, which is the standard height for a net used in table tennis.

The Pritchard family had a lot of fun participating in this new activity, which they called "paddle tennis." They eventually showed the game to their friends, including Bill Bell, who became interested in it. Bell recognized the potential of the game and contributed to the improvement of the rules as well as the equipment.

The first ever pickleball court was built in 1967 in the backyard of Pritchard's neighbor, Barney McCallum. McCallum had a significant role in advancing the sport and was essential in the formation of the first pickleball club in the Seattle area.

Development of the Game

In the years that followed when it started, the sport of pickleball underwent continuous development. The paddles used in the game were initially constructed of plywood, but players quickly began experimenting with various materials, such as aluminum and graphite. Graphite, composite materials, and wood are just few of the materials that are used in the making of pickleball paddles in today's world.

The ball that is used in pickleball has also evolved over the course of its history. The first ball was a perforated plastic ball that was about the same size as a wiffle ball. The modern pickleball is a little bit larger and has holes that are a little bit smaller than they used to be. This helps to lessen the amount of wind resistance and provides better control.

In addition, the rules of pickleball have been perfected over the course of its history. Players were permitted to volley the ball from any location on the court when the sport was first being played. Today, there are specific rules regarding where a player can volley the ball and when they are allowed to do so.

Modifications have also been made during the course of its history to the pickleball scoring system. In the beginning of the game, participants would compete to a total of 21 points, and the winner was determined by whoever won by a margin of two points. These days, the majority of games are played to 11 points, but the winner still needs to triumph by a margin of two points.

Pickleball Today

Pickleball has grown to become a widely popular sport that is now played not only in all 50 states of the United States but also in many other nations all over the world. The United States of America Pickleball Association (USAPA) serves as the regulatory organization for the sport in the country, and it is responsible for establishing rules, equipment requirements, and tournament guidelines.

One of the factors that has contributed to pickleball's rapid rise in popularity over the past few years is the fact that it is a sport with a low risk of injury and is suitable for players of varying ages and degrees of expertise. It is less physically taxing than sports such as tennis or basketball due to the smaller court size and slower ball speed, thus it is an excellent option for older people or individuals who have joint difficulties.

Pickleball is not only popular as a sport, but also as a social activity, as evidenced by the increasing number of pickleball classes, clinics, and competitions among various clubs and organizations. The culture of the sport is warm and inviting, which has contributed to the sport's success in attracting a wide variety of players.

In recent years, pickleball has also gained popularity as a competitive sport. There have been an increasing number of events that provide financial awards, which has attracted the best players from all over the world. One of the most important and prominent pickleball tournaments in the world is the USAPA National Championships, which takes place every year in November in the United States.

In conclusion, the sport of pickleball is relatively new, but it has seen a meteoric rise in popularity over the past several years. It was initially played on a badminton court using homemade equipment when it was first played in 1965 by Joel Pritchard and Bill Bell, who were the inventors of the game. The sport progressed over the course of time, and as a result, it is now played on a more condensed court with specialized paddles and balls.

The sport of pickleball has risen in popularity for a number of different reasons, including the fact that it has a low impact, the fact that it has a social culture, and the fact that it offers competitive opportunities. The game keeps expanding and advancing, and it is now played in all fifty states as well as in a large number of other countries all over the world. There has never been a better time to give pickleball a shot, regardless of whether you are a beginner player or an experienced player, as there has never been a better time to see what all the excitement is about with this sport.

Benefits of playing pickleball

The sports of tennis, badminton, and ping pong are the foundation for the game of pickleball, which is a combination of all three. It is played on a court that is significantly smaller, with a ball made of perforated plastic, and paddles. Pickleball, in addition to being a fun and thrilling sport, has numerous positive effects on both one's health and social life.

The fact that playing pickleball is a low-impact type of exercise is one of the most significant advantages associated with the sport. Because of the shorter court length and slower ball speed, it is a sport that requires less physical work than others such as tennis and basketball. Because of this, it is an excellent choice for individuals who may have issues with their joints or other physical restrictions.

Pickleball still counts as a fantastic cardiovascular workout despite the fact that it is a low-impact sport. Players are required to maintain consistent movement throughout the court, which helps to raise their heart rate and burn more calories. Pickleball is a form of exercise that can be beneficial for both weight loss and the maintenance of a healthy weight, since it can burn up to 600 calories in one hour of play, as stated by the American Council on Exercise.

Pickleball is another sport that involves a significant amount of coordination and balance. The ability to move rapidly and change direction without losing one's balance is a requirement for players, and it contributes to an improvement in general body control.

Studies have shown that engaging in regular physical activity can help to improve balance and lower the chance of falling, making this an especially helpful practice for senior citizens. In point of fact, according to the findings of a study that was published in the Journal of Aging and Physical Activity, just eight weeks of playing pickleball led to significant improvements in the leg strength and balance of older people.

Pickleball is a sport that involves a high level of physical activity and frequent movement, both of which can assist enhance one's cardiovascular health. Exercising on a consistent basis has been found to lower one's risk of developing chronic health issues such as heart disease, stroke, and others.

Adults should strive to get at least 150 minutes of exercise per week at a moderate level, as recommended by the American Heart Association, in order to keep their cardiovascular systems in good shape. Pickleball can help you reach this goal while also providing a fun and engaging way to stay active for just 30 minutes a day, three times a week.

Pickleball is a sport that not only has great effects on a player's physical health, but also on their mental and emotional well-being. Exercising has been demonstrated to lessen the symptoms of both anxiety and depression, and it also has the potential to help improve cognitive performance.

Pickleball, in particular, has the potential to be an activity that brings people together, keeps them engaged, and helps to relieve stress and enhance mood. Playing pickleball with other people can be an effective way to counteract feelings of loneliness and isolation, and this is especially true for older persons, who are more likely to be at risk of being socially isolated.

Pickleball is a sport that is played in teams, making it a great way to meet new people and strengthen a sense of community. A great number of pickleball clubs and organizations host workshops, clinics, and competitions that bring together players of all skill levels and allow them to meet new people and make new friends.

This is especially helpful for older persons, who may be more likely to experience social isolation and loneliness as a result of their age. A study that was conducted on older persons and published in the Journal of Aging and Physical Activity indicated that participants in a pickleball program saw gains in both their social connectedness and their perceived social support.

Pickleball also has the potential to present players with possibilities for competition and accomplishment. There are a lot of pickleball events, and many of them provide cash prizes, which draw the best players from all over the world. This might serve as a source of inspiration for players who have the objective of enhancing their abilities in order to compete at a higher level.

Keeping oneself motivated and focused on one's fitness goals can also be made more enjoyable and interesting through the usage of healthy competition. Exercise routines can benefit from having a sense of organization and purpose, as well as a sense of accomplishment and pride in one's talents, when these elements are included.

Players in pickleball need to immediately track and react to the motions of the ball in order to be successful. This helps to develop hand-eye coordination, which is a skill that is crucial in a wide variety of sports and activities that people participate in on a daily basis.

In addition to helping to enhance reaction speed and lower the risk of injury, having good hand-eye coordination can also help. Given that reaction times typically slow down with older age, this is of utmost significance for senior citizens.

Pickleball offers an additional advantage in that it may be played in either an indoor or outdoor setting. This gives players a greater degree of flexibility and variety in the alternatives available to them when playing.

Courts that are played on outside can be found in places like parks and leisure areas, while courts that are played on indoors can be found in places like gymnasiums and community centers. Participating in activities outside can bring extra health benefits, such as increased exposure to sunlight and unpolluted air.

Pickleball is a sport that can be enjoyed by people of all ages and ability levels, which is one of the reasons why it is so popular. Another reason pickleball is so appealing is that it is a sport that can be played inside. The game is easily adaptable to accommodate players of varying levels, and it allows players to set their own pace while they play.

Because of this, it is a great sport for families, as both adults and children of varying skill levels are able to compete against one another in the same game. It is also a popular sport among senior citizens, who may be looking for a low-impact activity that can help them remain active and engaged throughout their later years.

In conclusion, pickleball is a sport that is not only enjoyable but also engaging, and it offers numerous benefits to both one's physical health and social life. People of various ages and skill levels are drawn to the game for a variety of reasons, including the fact that it is a low-impact form of exercise, the social connections that can be made, and the opportunity for competitiveness.

Pickleball can be an enjoyable and gratifying method to stay active and enhance both your general health and well-being. This is true regardless of whether you are an experienced athlete or someone who is just beginning to explore the world of fitness. Grab a paddle, locate a court, and get ready to be blown away by everything that the beautiful sport of pickleball has to offer you.

Chapter I

Equipment

Overview of necessary equipment

A sport known as pickleball has seen significant growth in popularity during the past several years. It is played on a court that is significantly smaller, with a ball made of perforated plastic, and paddles. Pickleball is a sport that can be played by just about anyone, but it does require a certain amount of specialized gear in order to participate.

When it comes to playing pickleball, the paddle is the one most important piece of equipment. The paddle is what is used to hit the ball, and it can be manufactured out of a number of different materials, such as wood, graphite, or composite materials.

Paddles made of wood are not only the oldest and most popular option, but they also tend to be the most affordable. They are long-lasting and offer a satisfactory level of control, but they are also the heaviest of the available choices. Graphite paddles are more expensive, but they are lighter, offer better control, and are more powerful. Paddles that are composed of composite materials are made from a combination of several materials, and they give a good balance of control, power, and durability.

When selecting for a paddle, you should give careful consideration to your playing style, degree of expertise, and financial constraints. Because a decent paddle can assist to improve your game, it is important to make an investment in a paddle that is of high quality and satisfies all of your requirements.

Pickleball uses a ball that is comparable in size to a wiffle ball and is perforated to lessen the amount of air resistance it presents to the player. There is a wide variety of ball colors available for play in pickleball, but the yellow ball is the most common.

It is essential to take into consideration the pickleball court that you will be playing on when choosing a ball for the game. Indoor balls are often softer and less likely to damage indoor court surfaces, in contrast to outdoor balls, which are typically more durable and have a greater hardness rating.

It is also essential to take into account the difficulty of the game. It's possible that novice players would choose a ball that's simpler to control and that's softer, while more experienced players could favor a ball that's harder and has more power and speed.

Courts for the sport of pickleball are typically smaller than tennis courts and are approximately the same size as badminton courts. The dimensions of a typical pickleball court are 20 feet wide by 44 feet long.

A net that is 36 inches high around the edges of the court and 34 inches high in the middle of the court serves to divide the court in half. The court also contains a non-volley zone, which is a 7-foot space on each side of the net where players are not permitted to hit the ball in the air.

It is possible to play pickleball on a tennis court that has been modified or on another surface; however, in order to get the most out of the game, it is recommended that you play on a court that is the standard size.

Pickleball is just like any other sport because it requires players to have appropriate footwear. Shoes designed for pickleball should offer adequate support, cushioning, and traction for the sport.

It is essential to take into consideration the kind of pickleball court surface you will be playing on when selecting a pair of pickleball shoes. If you're playing on an indoor court, go for shoes with a gum sole, and if you're playing on an outdoor court, look for shoes with a hard sole.

In addition to this, it is essential that you select shoes that have a decent fit and offer adequate support for your feet and ankles. Both having shoes that are too tight and having shoes that are too loose can be uncomfortable and can raise the risk of injury.

When it comes to playing pickleball, the most important pieces of equipment are the paddle, the ball, the court, and the shoes; however, there are a few more things that players could find useful.

One example of this kind of item is a pickleball bag, which is designed to hold and transport several pieces of equipment, such as paddles, balls, and other accessories. Pickleball bags are available in a wide range of sizes and designs, and they can be an effective and simple method to store and transport your equipment.

A pickleball net system is another useful piece of equipment, as it enables players to construct a pickleball court virtually anyplace. It is possible to get portable net systems that are suitable for use either indoors or outdoors and that are simple to set up and take down. This enables the sport of pickleball to be played in a number of settings, including parks, schools, and community centers, among other places.

When playing pickleball, it is essential that players wear clothes that is suited for the sport. The ideal attire is loose-fitting, breathable, and comfortable, and it should not restrict movement in any way. The majority of players will compete in their chosen sporting attire, which typically consists of shorts, t-shirts, and tennis shoes.

Finally, it is essential to pack water or other liquids that can help you stay hydrated in order to ensure that you do not become dehydrated while playing. Pickleball may be a sport that puts a player through a lot of physical demand; therefore, players should be sure to drink enough fluids to avoid becoming dehydrated.

In conclusion, in order to play pickleball, you are going to need some basic equipment, such as a paddle, a ball, a court, and shoes. It is essential that you select gear that is suitable for your current level of expertise, playing style, and financial constraints.

A pickleball bag, a net system, and clothing that is suited for the sport are some examples of additional items that might be helpful when playing pickleball in addition to the necessary equipment that is required.

Players are able to take part in a game that is not only entertaining and interesting but also has a number of positive effects on their health and their ability to interact with others. Pick up your paddle, your ball, and any other equipment you'll need, and get ready to enjoy all of the fun and excitement that pickleball has to offer.

How to select a paddle

A sport known as pickleball has seen significant growth in interest during the past several years. It is played on a court that is significantly smaller, with a ball made of perforated plastic, and paddles. Pickleball is played with a paddle, which is the most important piece of equipment because it is used for hitting the ball during play.

When selecting for a pickleball paddle, the first thing you should take into consideration is the material it's constructed of. Wood, graphite, or composite materials are the most common materials used in the manufacture of paddles.

Paddles made of wood are not only the most traditional alternative, but they are also often the most affordable. They are long-lasting and offer a satisfactory level of control, but they are also the heaviest of the available choices. Beginner players who are just beginning the sport of pickleball might consider using paddles made of wood as their preferred material.

Graphite paddles are more powerful and offer greater control than wooden paddles, but they are much lighter. They are more expensive, but not only are they more durable but they also have a longer potential lifespan. Players of an intermediate or advanced skill level who are searching for better performance may want to consider using graphite paddles.

Paddles composed of composite materials, such as graphite and fiberglass, are constructed using a combination of the two materials. They provide a perfect balance of control, power, and durability in their products. Players who are looking for a paddle that can serve a variety of purposes and is versatile might consider purchasing a composite paddle.

When picking a pickleball paddle, the weight of the paddle is another vital component to take into consideration. The average weight of a paddle can range anywhere from 6 to 14 ounces.

Paddles that are lighter are easier to manipulate and provide more control, but they may not have as much power as heavier paddles. There is a trade-off between increased power and increased difficulty in paddling with heavier paddles.

Your individual tastes and playing style will determine the weight of the paddle that is best suited for you to use. Players who are just starting out may like a lighter paddle because it is simpler to manage, while players who are more experienced may favor a heavier paddle because it generates more force.

A pickleball paddle's grip size is another key aspect to think about before purchasing one. The circumference of the handle, which is referred to as the grip size, can be anything from 4 and 5 inches.

It is possible for a grip that is too small to produce discomfort and lead to a loss of control, while a grip that is too large can lead to fatigue and a loss of power. It is essential to select a grip size that not only feels good in the hand but also offers a high level of control and power.

The distance between your palm and the end of your middle finger is the distance that should be measured to establish the appropriate size of the grip. Utilizing this measurement, you will be able to choose the grip size that is most suitable for your paddle.

When choosing a pickleball paddle, the shape of the paddle is another issue that should be taken into consideration. Standard and widebody are the two primary forms that paddles can take.

Widebody paddles have a larger sweet spot and have a larger hitting surface than standard paddles. They are a smart purchase for novice players who are still honing their abilities and are a good option overall.

The hitting surface of a standard paddle is significantly smaller, which results in improved control and precision. They are an excellent option for more experienced players who are searching for improved overall performance.

When choosing a paddle, the amount of noise that it makes is another issue to take into consideration. When some paddles hit the ball, the sound they make might be annoying to other players because it is audible.

It is essential to select a paddle that does not make an excessive amount of noise and does not produce an excessive amount of volume. This can be determined by using a variety of paddles and paying attention to the sounds they produce as they make contact with the ball during practice.

When choosing a pickleball paddle, it's important to also consider about how much money you are willing to spend on one. There is a wide price range for paddles, from less than $20 to over $200 per unit.

Although it could be tempting to go with a less expensive paddle, it is essential to make the financial investment in a high-quality paddle that is suited to your requirements. Your performance and the overall quality of the game can both benefit from the use of a high-quality paddle. It is important to purchase a paddle that is not only long-lasting but also easy to handle and fits to your own tastes.

The ideal method to choose a pickleball paddle is to try out a few different paddles and determine which one provides you with the most comfortable feel while still satisfying your requirements. Paddle demos are available at a variety of sports goods stores and pickleball facilities, and they provide customers the opportunity to test out a variety of paddles before making a purchase.

When evaluating paddles, it is essential to take into account their price, noise level, grip size, and shape in addition to the material they are made of. It is also essential to take into account the preferences and playing style that are unique to you.

In conclusion, when it comes to playing pickleball, choosing the appropriate paddle to use is an essential step. When choosing a paddle, it is essential to think about the material it is made of, how much it weighs, how big the grip is, what form it has, how loud it is, and how much it costs. It is also essential to try out a variety of paddles to see which one provides the best comfort level and best satisfies your requirements.

Your performance and the overall quality of the game can both benefit from the use of a high-quality paddle. Purchasing a high-quality paddle that caters to both your individual preferences and the way you want to play the game is a good investment that can help you get more enjoyment out of playing the game.

Choosing the right ball

In recent years, there has been a meteoric rise in the number of people playing the sport of pickleball. It is played on a court that is significantly smaller, with a ball made of perforated plastic, and paddles. When it comes to playing pickleball, the paddle is by far the most significant piece of equipment; however, the ball is also an essential component.

When choosing for a pickleball ball, the first thing you should take into consideration is the material it's constructed of. The balls used in pickleball are typically manufactured of plastic and can come in a number of various densities.

Because of their lower density, low-density balls are softer and move at a slower pace, making them an ideal choice for novice players. They are less difficult to maintain control over and offer a more leisurely pace of play, both of which can assist players in the process of skill development.

The majority of players can benefit from using balls with a density that falls somewhere in the middle of the spectrum. They are a wonderful option for players who are searching for a ball that can be used effectively in a variety of situations since they provide a harmony between control and power.

Because of their greater toughness and increased speed, balls with a high density are an excellent option for more experienced players. Players who want the game to go at a faster pace can consider using them because they give greater power and speed and are an excellent option overall.

When choosing a ball density, it is essential to take into account both your individual preferences and the way you play the game. It's possible that novice players would prefer a ball with a lower density because it's simpler to manage, while more experienced players could favor a ball with a higher density because it offers more power and speed.

There is a variety of color options available for the balls used in pickleball, including yellow, white, and neon. Yellow is by far the most common color for pickleball balls, though white and neon balls are also available.

The yellow balls are the easiest to spot, making them the optimal option for the vast majority of players. They are easy to spot on the court and give enough visibility in a number of different lighting scenarios.

White balls are less noticeable and can be difficult to spot, particularly in environments with low levels of available light. They are a fantastic option for activity that takes place indoors, where the lighting is typically bright.

Players who want a ball that stands out might consider using neon balls because of their great visibility and because they are a fantastic choice overall. They are an excellent option for playing outside and are able to be seen clearly even when the sun is shining brightly.

When choosing a color for the ball, it is essential to take into consideration the lighting circumstances as well as the color of the court. The yellow balls are the most adaptable and are an excellent option for the majority of different playing settings.

When selecting a ball for pickleball, another element to take into consideration is how long the ball will last. The density of the pickleball ball as well as the components it is made out of can have an effect on how long it will last.

Balls with a lower density often have a shorter lifespan and can experience greater levels of wear and tear than balls with a higher density. It's possible that they'll need to be replaced more regularly, which can rack up additional expenses over time.

Balls with a higher density are often more durable and can continue to function for a longer period of time than balls with a lower density. They are more resistant to wear and tear, therefore it is possible that they will not need to be replaced as regularly.

When choosing a ball based on its durability, it is essential to take into account both the intensity of the gameplay and the number of times it will be used. Beginner players may choose a lower-density ball because it is simpler to handle and because it needs to be replaced more frequently. Advanced players who play the game on a regular basis may prefer a ball with a higher density because it is more durable.

When choosing a pickleball ball, you need also take into consideration how much money you are willing to spend. The cost of a single ball can range anywhere from less than one dollar to more than three dollars.

Although it may be tempting to go with a less expensive ball, it is essential to make the investment in a high-quality ball that fits to your requirements. Your performance and the overall quality of the game can both benefit from the use of a high-quality ball.

When choosing a ball based on price, it is essential to take into consideration the level of play and the number of times it will be used. Beginner players might prefer a cheaper ball that is simpler to replace more frequently, while advanced players who play more frequently might prefer a more expensive ball that is more durable and performs better.

The easiest approach to choose which ball is best for you to use when playing pickleball is to try out a few different balls and see which one provides the most comfortable experience. Ball demos are available at a variety of sporting goods stores and pickleball facilities, and they provide customers the opportunity to try out a variety of balls before making a purchase.

When evaluating balls, it is essential to think about their density as well as their color, durability, and cost. It is essential that you take into account the lighting circumstances as well as the surface color of the court.

In summary, when it comes to playing pickleball, selecting the appropriate ball is an essential component. When selecting a ball, it is vital to think about the material it is made of, the color, how long it will last, and how much it will cost. It is essential that you try out a variety of balls to see which one provides the optimal level of comfort for you.

Your performance and the overall quality of the game can both benefit from the use of a high-quality ball. Your enjoyment of the game can be improved by making a worthwhile investment in a high-quality ball that is tailored to your own preferences as well as the way you want to play the game.

When choosing a ball, it is essential to take into account your individual tastes, the degree of your talent, and the playing style you choose. Regardless of whether you are a novice or an experienced player, selecting the appropriate ball can have a significant impact on the overall experience and pleasure you gain from playing the game. Grab a ball and get ready to have a blast as you discover everything that the sport of pickleball has to offer in terms of fun and excitement.

Court layout and dimensions

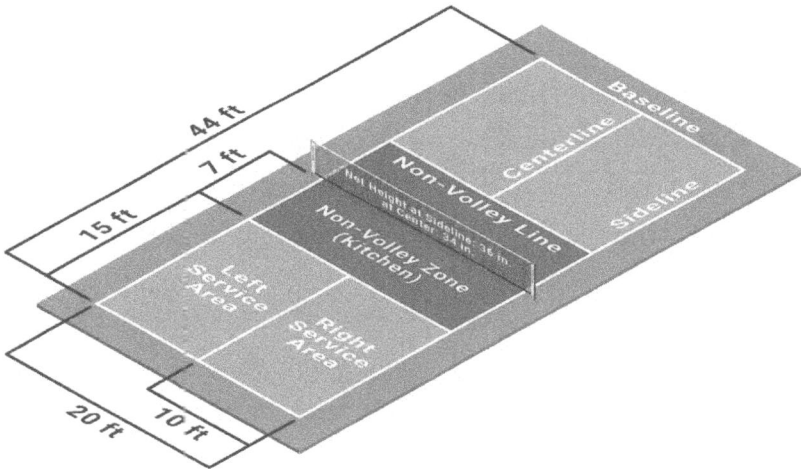

Pickleball is a sport that is both exciting and fun to play, and in recent years it has seen a rise in its level of popularity. In comparison to regular tennis, it is played on a court that is significantly smaller, and the size of the court are extremely important to the gameplay.

It is necessary for players to have a thorough understanding of the court layout of a pickleball court in order to comprehend the limits and different areas of the court. The dimensions of the court, including the sidelines, are 44 feet in length and 20 feet in width. The court is rectangular in design. A net runs along the length of the court, dividing it in half and then subdividing each half into two separate zones.

The first region of the court is the non-volley zone, also referred to as the kitchen because of its proximity to the baseline. It is a 7-foot-deep area that is situated away from the net on both sides of the court. Players are not permitted to volley the ball while they are standing inside the kitchen, which is marked by a line that is 2 inches wide. It is necessary for the player to leave the kitchen in order to hit a ball that will bounce inside the kitchen. Only after leaving the kitchen can the player then return to hit the ball.

The service area is the second part of the court and can be found directly behind the non-volley zone on both sides of the court. A 2-inch-wide line designates the service area, which is a 10-foot-deep area from the net. The players are required to serve the ball from this region in order to begin the game or to continue play once a point has been scored.

Players are required to have an understanding of the many markings that are located on a pickleball court in addition to the dimensions of the court itself. The court is split in half along the centerline, which is a line that is perpendicular to the net and runs the length of the court. The service area is a rectangle measuring 10 feet by 15 feet and is located behind the non-volley zone. The centerline is also used to identify the service area.

In addition, the service area is denoted by the service line, which has a width of 2 inches and is oriented in a direction that is parallel to the net. When serving, the ball must land within a certain area, which is marked by the service line, which is 15 feet away from the net. When a player is serving, they are required to stand behind the service line, and they must strike the serve underhand with the paddle below their waist.

The non-volley zone, also known as the kitchen, is a rectangle that measures 7 feet by 20 feet and is located on both sides of the court. It is marked by a line that is 2 inches wide and runs along the non-volley zone. It is against the rules for players to volley the ball while they are standing inside the kitchen, and any ball that lands inside the kitchen must be played outside the kitchen.

The outer borders of the court, known as the sidelines and baselines, are marked by lines that are 2 inches wide. The sidelines are aligned in a direction that is parallel to the net, while the baselines are aligned in a direction that is perpendicular to the net. The sidelines and baselines are 20 feet and 44 feet, respectively, in dimensions.

It is necessary to have certain pieces of equipment in order to play pickleball, in addition to having the court laid out and sized correctly. The net is an important piece of equipment, and it must be set up properly before the game can begin. The sidelines of the court have a net that is 36 inches high, while the center of the court has a net that is 34 inches high. It is held in place by two poles that are spaced at the conventional distance of 22 feet apart, which is the width of a pickleball court.

Pickleball's most essential piece of gear is the paddle, which may be purchased in a wide variety of materials, shapes, and dimensions. Wood, graphite, and composite are the three kinds of material that are most frequently used to make paddles. According to the rules of the USA Pickleball Association, the paddle can be no larger than 24 inches in length, 8 inches in width, and no more than 1 inch in thickness at any point. These dimensions are the maximum allowed for the paddle.

Pickleball is played with a ball made of perforated plastic that is slightly larger than a tennis ball. This ball is utilized in the game. The ball is available in a wide variety of colors, densities, and sizes. Pickleball's most frequent ball is the indoor ball, which is smaller, has larger holes, and weighs less than the outside ball. The wind resistance of the outdoor ball is increased due to its increased weight and its smaller hole size. The choice of ball should be made with consideration for the playing surface, the current weather, and the player's own preferences.

Players are required to adhere to the rules of the game in addition to having a grasp of the layout and dimensions of the court and have the appropriate equipment. The USA Pickleball Association is responsible for establishing the game's rules, and these guidelines are modified on a regular basis to guarantee that everyone has an equal opportunity to win.

The double-bounce rule is considered to be one of the most important rules in pickleball. According to this rule, a player is not allowed to volley the ball until the ball has first been allowed to bounce once on either side of the net. The regulation that requires players to double-bounce the ball both slows down the pace of the game and makes it accessible to players of varying skill levels.

One more important rule in pickleball is known as the "non-volley zone rule." According to this rule, players are not allowed to volley the ball when they are standing in the kitchen area. Before playing a ball that bounces inside the kitchen, players are required to exit the kitchen and move to a safe distance.

When serving the ball, players are required to adhere to the service regulations as well. Underhand serving is required, and the paddle must be held below the player's waist at all times. The serve has to go into the service area of the opponent, and the server has to be behind the line that denotes the service area.

When it comes to playing pickleball, the court's dimensions and layout are two of the most important considerations. The dimensions of the court are 44 feet in length and 20 feet in width, while the height of the net is 36 inches at the sides and 34 inches in the middle of the court. There is a net that runs down the middle of the court, dividing it in half, and inside each half, there are two distinct areas: the non-volley zone and the service area.

When playing pickleball, having the appropriate equipment is also absolutely necessary. The ball is available in a wide variety of densities, colors, and sizes, while the paddles can be made of a variety of materials and come in a variety of shapes and sizes.

To be successful at pickleball, it is necessary to have a good understanding of the court's layout and dimensions, to have the appropriate equipment, and to abide by the rules of the game. Your ability to play the game well and avoid making mistakes is directly correlated to your familiarity with the rules of the game as well as the boundaries of the court. This is true whether you are a novice or an experienced player.

Pickleball is a sport that is not only entertaining and thrilling but also provides a terrific way to get in shape and interact with others. It is simple to pick up, and people of many ages and levels of expertise can enjoy playing it. Pickleball is a sport that is filled with a lot of fun and excitement, so gather a friend, a paddle, and get ready to enjoy everything that this sport has to offer.

Chapter II

Rules of the Game

Scoring system

Pickleball is a sport that is experiencing expanding levels of popularity all over the world. It is a sport that is played at a fast-paced and incorporates aspects of tennis, badminton, and ping pong. The court is reduced in size, and there is a lower net and a specialized ball used in the game. Pickleball has a scoring system that is unique compared to those of other sports; hence, it is vital to have an understanding of this scoring system in order to play the game correctly.

Each participant in a game of pickleball uses a paddle in order to hit a plastic ball over a net and into the court of their opponent. This can be done in either a singles or a doubles setting. The goal of the game is to rack up points by hitting the ball in a way that prevents the other player from receiving it back. The game is won by the first team to reach 11 points while also holding at least a two-point lead over the other team.

When a rally is won by the team that is serving, those points are scored. A rally occurs when one team serves the ball to the other and both teams hit it back and forth over the net until one team is unable to return the ball, at this point the score is awarded to the other team.

Depending on the skill level of the players and the rules of the competition, a match will normally be played to the best of three or five sets. When there are three games played, the winner of the match is determined by whose team wins the first two games. When there are five games played, the winner of the match is determined by which team wins three of them first.

When playing singles, each player will take turns serving the ball, and a coin toss will be used to determine who will serve first at the beginning of each game. The person who emerges victorious from the toss of the coin will have the option of either serving or receiving the serve for the first game. The person who is serving gets two chances to hit the ball into the court of their opponent; if they are unsuccessful, the serve is given to the opponent.

One point is awarded to the player who wins the serve in a match. If the player who was receiving the ball wins the rally, the person who was receiving the ball becomes the player who is serving, and the score keeps the same. If the player who is serving comes out on top in the rally, they are awarded a point and get to keep serving.

When playing singles, the person who is serving must hit the ball in a diagonal direction across the court, beginning on the right side of the court. The serve has to end up in the service court of the opponent, and it has to go over the non-volley zone, also known as the kitchen. In the event that the serve does not fulfill these standards, the attempt is regarded as a fault, and the opposing player receives the opportunity to serve.

When playing doubles, both players on a team take turns serving, and the team that is serving rotates positions after each point. A toss of the coin is used to determine who will serve the first point of each game, and the team that wins the toss gets to select whether they will serve or receive the point for the first game.

The team that is serving is required to serve in a direction that is diagonal across the court, beginning on the right side of the court. The serve has to end up in the service court of the opponent, and it has to go over the non-volley zone, also known as the kitchen. In the event that the serve does not fulfill these standards, the attempt is regarded as a fault, and the opposing player receives the opportunity to serve.

A point is awarded to the team that is victorious in the serve. If the team that was receiving points wins the rally, the team that was receiving points becomes the team that is serving, and the score stays the same. If the team that is serving wins in the rally, not only do they score a point but they also keep serving.

The "two-bounce" rule is one of the rules that can be used in doubles. According to this rule, following the serve, each team is required to let the ball bounce at least once on their own side of the court before returning it to the opposing team. After the ball has been allowed to bounce on both sides, players are allowed to hit the ball without allowing it to bounce again.

When a team reaches 11 points and has a lead of at least two points, that team automatically wins the game. In the event that the score is tied at 10-10, play will continue until one team has a two-point advantage over the other. The highest possible score in this game is 15, and the margin of victory must be at least two points.

When playing doubles, players switch places on the court at various intervals. After each point, the players on both teams exchange positions, with the player who was at the net going to the back of the court and the player who was at the back moving to the net. The player on the right-hand side of the court serves the ball for the first point, and after each point, the player who was at the net serves the ball for the next point.

The scoring system in pickleball can be difficult to understand for newcomers, and players frequently make mistakes when attempting to use it. Forgetting to announce the score is one of the most typical mistakes that people make. Before each serve, the players should communicate the score to each other, starting with the score of the team that is serving and moving on to the score of the team that is receiving.

Another typical oversight is failing to remember the "two-bounce" rule when playing doubles. After the serve, the players on either side of the court are obligated to let the ball bounce at least once on their end of the court before passing it to the opposing team.

Players should also be aware of errors like serving into the wrong court, failing to volley the ball over the net, or standing in the non-volley zone while volleying the ball. These errors lead to the loss of the serve, which gives the other team the opportunity to earn a point.

In conclusion, it is absolutely necessary to have a solid understanding of the pickleball scoring system in order to play the game correctly. When playing singles, each player will take turns serving the ball, and a coin toss will be used to determine who will serve first at the beginning of each game. The player who is serving is required to serve in a direction that is diagonal across the court, beginning on the right side of the court. When playing doubles, both players on a team take turns serving, and the team that serves must move their ball in a diagonal direction across the court, beginning on the right side of the court.

It is only possible to score points if the team that is serving does so successfully, and most matches are played to the best of three or five points, depending on the difficulty of the game and the regulations of the tournament. Pickleball's scoring system might be difficult to understand for newcomers, but if players take the time to familiarize themselves with the fundamentals of the game and steer clear of the most common errors, they can find pleasure in playing and enhance their abilities.

Pickleball is a sport that is not only entertaining and thrilling but also provides a terrific way to get in shape and interact with others. Understanding the scoring system is vital to playing the game of pickleball and getting the most out of all the opportunities that the sport of pickleball has to offer, regardless of whether you are a novice or an experienced player. Pickleball is a sport that is filled with a lot of fun and excitement, so gather a friend, a paddle, and get ready to enjoy everything that this sport has to offer!

Serving rules

Pickleball is a sport that combines elements of tennis, badminton, and ping pong, and it is a very enjoyable and thrilling sport. It is played on a court that is far smaller, with a net that is significantly lower, and a unique ball. Serving is an important part of pickleball since it is how the ball is first placed into play at the beginning of each rally.

In pickleball, the ball is first put into play through the process known as "serving." To begin the rally, the team that is serving must first send the ball to the team that is receiving it, and the team that is receiving it must then send the ball back over the net. The team that is serving is required to serve in a direction that is diagonal across the court, beginning on the right side of the court.

The serve has to end up in the service court of the opponent, and it has to go over the non-volley zone, also known as the kitchen. In the event that the serve does not fulfill these standards, the attempt is regarded as a fault, and the opposing player receives the opportunity to serve.

Understanding the rules of serving is vital for having a successful game of pickleball because the serve is such an integral component of the overall experience.

When playing singles, each player will take turns serving the ball, and a coin toss will be used to determine who will serve first at the beginning of each game. The person who emerges victorious from the toss of the coin will have the option of either serving or receiving the serve for the first game. The person who is serving gets two opportunities to hit the ball into the court of their opponent; if they are unsuccessful, the serve is given to the opponent.

The player who is serving is required to make their serve in a diagonal direction across the court, beginning on the right side of the court. The serve has to end up in the service court of the opponent, and it has to go over the non-volley zone, also known as the kitchen. In the event that the serve does not meet these standards, the attempt is regarded as a fault, and the opposing player receives the opportunity to serve.

Before the ball has been hit, the player who is serving is not allowed to walk over the kitchen line or touch the line that denotes the non-volley zone. If the player who is serving commits this mistake, it is considered a fault, and the other player receives the opportunity to serve.

When playing doubles, both players on a team take turns serving, and the team that is serving rotates positions after each point. A flip of the coin is used to determine who will serve the first point of each game, and the team that wins the toss gets to select whether they will serve or receive the point for the first game.

The team that is serving is required to serve in a direction that is diagonal across the court, beginning on the right side of the court. The serve has to end up in the service court of the opponent, and it has to go over the non-volley zone, also known as the kitchen. In the case that the serve does not fulfill these standards, the attempt is regarded as a fault, and the opposing player receives the opportunity to serve.

The team that is serving is responsible for following the proper order, which begins with the player who is located on the right side of the court serving the first point. Following the completion of each point, the players on both teams trade positions, with the player who was most recently stationed at the net moving to the back of the court, and the player who was most recently stationed at the back of the court moving to the net.

When the requirements of the serving rules are not satisfied by the serve, this is referred to as a fault. A let serve occurs when the ball touches the net when the player is serving, but the ball still lands in the correct service court. In this scenario, the serve is replayed, and the previous attempt is not counted as a fault.

Mistakes such as serving into the incorrect court, failing to hit the ball over the net, or volleying the ball while standing inside the non-volley zone are examples of some of the most common mistakes. These errors lead to the loss of the serve, which gives the other team the opportunity to earn a point.

It is also possible for the ball to be considered a let serve if it collides with an obstruction or another player before arriving in the appropriate service court. In this scenario, the serve is replayed, and the previous attempt is not counted as a fault.

In pickleball, players are required to adhere to a set of particular rules regarding the serving process. The following are some of the most important rules that should be kept in mind:

Before beginning to serve, the server is required to position themselves behind the baseline and within the service area. This rule guarantees that the server is in the appropriate position and is not trying to get an unfair advantage by standing too far in front of the service area or outside of it.

The second rule is that the server is not allowed to walk into the non-volley zone or touch the kitchen line before the ball has been hit. Players are reminded against entering the "kitchen line" because it is an important part of the court and doing so would result in a violation of the rules. Players are required to wait until the ball has rebounded before entering the non-volley zone since it is a vital part of the game.

Thirdly, the ball must be hit with the paddle at a level that is lower than the player's waist. This rule prevents the server from trying to gain an edge over the receiving team by hitting the ball with an excessive amount of force or from an unfavorable angle, both of which are prohibited by the rule.

The fourth point is that the server is required to wait until the receiver is ready before beginning service. This rule ensures that both teams are prepared to receive the serve and that the competition is conducted in a fair manner. Players are not allowed to surprise their opponents with an unexpected serve or attempt to catch them off guard in any way.

The fifth rule is that the server must serve in a diagonal direction across the court, beginning on the right side of the court. Because of this rule, the person who is serving cannot intentionally aim the ball at their opponent or try to gain an unfair advantage by serving from the wrong side of the court.

The final requirement for a successful serve is that it must enter the service court of the opponent and pass through the "kitchen" or "non-volley zone". This rule ensures that the serve is played properly and that the team that receives the ball has an equal opportunity to return the ball to the server.

It is essential to keep in mind that in order to score a point, the team that is serving must win the rally. If the team that was receiving wins the rally, the team that was receiving becomes the team that is serving, and the score stays the same. If the team that is serving wins in the rally, not only do they score a point but they also keep serving.

Faults and violations

Tennis, badminton, and ping pong are all included in the fun and exciting game of pickleball. It is played on a court that is far smaller, with a net that is significantly lower, and a special ball. Playing by the rules is one of the most important aspects of pickleball, and there are particular faults and violations that players must stay away of to guarantee that the game is played fairly.

When a player or team in a game of pickleball does not adhere to the game's rules, faults and violations can occur. In the event of a fault, the player will lose either a point or the opportunity to serve, while violations will result in a warning and, in more serious scenarios, disqualification.

Serving the ball into the incorrect court, failing to hit the ball over the net, or volleying the ball while standing inside the non-volley zone are all examples of common faults that players make. These errors lead to the loss of the serve, which gives the other team the opportunity to earn a point.

Conduct that is seen to be unsportsmanlike, arguing with either the referee or an opponent, or interfering with a shot taken by an opponent are all examples of behaviors that might result in a violation. Depending on the seriousness of the violation, such offenses can result in a warning, a point deduction, or even disqualification from the competition.

It is necessary to keep in mind that pickleball is a game of integrity, and that players are expected to compete in a fair manner while demonstrating excellent sportsmanship.

When playing pickleball, one of the most common faults is to serve the ball into the incorrect court. The team that is serving is required to serve in a direction that is diagonal across the court, beginning on the right side of the court. If the ball is served into the incorrect court, this is termed a fault, and the other team will receive a point as a result.

Pickleball players often make the mistake of not hitting the ball high enough to get it over the net. In order for the shot to be declared successful, the ball needs to go over the net and into the court of the opponent. It is considered a fault, and the other team gets a point, if the ball does not successfully pass the net or if it lands outside of the playing area.

Players must avoid walking into the non-volley zone, which is often referred to as the kitchen, because it is a key region on the court and doing so will result in a fault being committed. In order to avoid making a fault when entering the non-volley zone, players are required to wait until the ball has bounced before doing so.

Another typical mistake is to volley the ball while standing in an area that is not permitted for volleying. Players are not allowed to hit the ball when they are standing in the area designated as the non-volley zone. If they do so, they will lose their serve and the other team will receive a point.

After the serve, the players on either side of the court are obligated to let the ball bounce at least once on their end of the court before passing it to the opposing team. If a player hits the ball before it has bounced twice, it is regarded as a fault, and the point will be awarded to the team that the player was playing against.

Unsportsmanlike conduct is a violation that happens when a player acts in a manner that is not in the spirit of the game. Unsportsmanlike conduct is a violation that can result in disqualification from the game. To argue with the referee or an opponent, mock them, or use language that is offensive are all examples of behavior that are not considered unsportsmanlike.

The players are not allowed to get in their opponent's way in any way while they are hitting. This includes actively trying to distract or block the vision or movement of their opponent, which might lead to a breach of the rule.

During the game, players are not allowed to touch the net in any way. It's possible that doing so will result in a violation, which will give the other team a point.

It is forbidden for players to strike the ball twice in a row. It is considered a violation when a player hits the ball two times in a row, which results in a point being awarded to the opposing team.

Players are only allowed to use their paddles to make contact with the ball; they are not allowed to carry or toss it. It's possible that doing so will result in a violation, which will give the other team a point.

During game play, players are not allowed to cross the centerline. It's possible that doing so will result in a violation, which will give the other team a point.

The severity of the violation determines the type and level of the penalty that is imposed for the fault or violation. In most situations, committing a fault will result in the loss of the serve, which will give the point to the other side. If the team that is serving commits a fault while serving, they will lose the serve, and the team that is receiving the serve will become the team that is serving.

Warnings, point deductions, or even disqualification are all possible outcomes for rule violations. For violations of a lesser severity, a warning may be issued, and the team that committed the violation may be obliged to lose a point. When a violation is considered more severe, further point deductions may be applied, and the team that committed the offense may be ordered to lose several points.

In the most severe of circumstances, one might be disqualified. A player is normally disqualified only in extreme circumstances, such as when they engage in behavior that is considered to be unsportsmanlike, regularly break the rules, or are thought to be a threat to either themselves or other players.

Playing singles and doubles

Pickleball is a sport that combines elements of tennis, badminton, and ping pong, and it is a very enjoyable and thrilling sport. It can be played in either a singles or doubles version, with both versions requiring a different set of techniques and a different set of rules.

Pickleball in the singles version is played between two players, with each player beginning the game on a different side of the court. The court dimensions for singles pickleball are the same as those for doubles pickleball, spanning 20 feet wide and 44 feet long.

When playing pickleball in a singles match, each player takes turns serving the ball, and the person who serves must do so in a diagonal direction across the court, beginning on the right side of the court. The player who wins in the rally is awarded a point, and the goal of the game is to accumulate 11 points, with a lead of two points being necessary to emerge victorious.

Players in singles pickleball are required to cover the entirety of the court. A common singles pickleball strategy involves hitting the ball to the opponent's weaker side or pushing them to travel around the court. Players also need to be conscious of their positioning on the court and should avoid standing in the non-volley zone unless it is absolutely necessary to hit a ball if they want to maximize their chances of success.

Due to the fact that they are the only one accountable for scoring points, players in singles pickleball are expected to be more aggressive and focused on racking up points as rapidly as possible. Players are required to execute a wide range of shots in order to score points and keep their opponents on their toes. These shots include groundstrokes, volleys, and overhead smashes.

When playing singles pickleball, hitting cross-court shots is one of the most effective technique you can use. Players can force their opponents to travel around the court and generate opportunities for winning shots by hitting the ball diagonally across the court. When hitting towards the opponent's weaker side with a cross-court shot, you will have a greater chance of success because this will make it more difficult for them to return the ball to you.

Utilizing the drop shot as part of your singles pickleball game plan is yet another effective strategy. The drop shot is a type of shot that is played delicately and lands just over the net. This causes the opponent to have to go closer to the ball in order to hit it. This can either set up a chance for a winning shot or compel the opponent to make a mistake that costs them the game. When used after a hard or deep shot, the drop shot is particularly effective because it can catch the opponent off guard and create an opening for the player to win the point.

The lob is a type of shot in which the ball is hit high above the head of the opponent. This causes the opponent to move away, which provides the player with more time to set up a winning stroke. When the opponent is at the net, lobs are highly effective because it can force them to go back, which in turn creates an opportunity for the player to hit a winning shot. Changing the pace of the game and maintaining the opponent's level of uncertainty can also be accomplished with lobs.

When playing doubles pickleball, there are two teams, each consisting of two players, and the players are positioned on opposite sides of the court. Both singles and doubles games of pickleball are played on courts that are 20 feet wide and 44 feet long.

In doubles pickleball, the serving team alternates serves after each point. The team that is serving is required to serve in a diagonal pattern across the court, beginning on the right side of the court. Additionally, the players on the serving team are required to switch positions after each point. The game is played to 11 points, and the winning side needs to have a lead of at least two points in order to claim victory. A point is awarded to the team that wins in the rally.

Players in a game of doubles pickleball need to work together as a team, talking with one another and coordinating their shots in order to cover the court and make it challenging for their opponents to return the ball. Players also need to be conscious of their positioning on the court and should avoid standing in the non-volley zone unless it is absolutely necessary to hit a ball if they want to maximize their chances of success.

Players need to have patience and be focused on setting up their partner for a winning shot when they are playing doubles pickleball. Players are required to keep their opponents on their toes by utilizing a variety of shots, such as groundstrokes, volleys, and overhead smashes. This will generate openings for winning shots and keep their opponents off balance.

The third shot drop is consistently regarded as one of the most successful strategy in doubles pickleball. The third shot drop is a shot that is hit gently and drops just over the net. This shot forces the opponent to move forward in order to hit the ball. Because of this, there is a chance that the team that is serving will have a chance to enter into the non-volley zone and take control of the point. When the serving side falls behind in the point, the third shot drop can be particularly useful because it can slow down the game and give them the opportunity to regain control of the situation.

Covering the middle of the court is an additional approach that can be utilized effectively in doubles pickleball. When playing doubles, it's common for one player to be near the net while the other stands at the baseline. It is important for the player who is guarding the net to cover the middle of the court, since this will make it more difficult for the other team to hit passing shots. When the net player covers the middle, they increase their chances of blocking shots and setting up their partner for successful shots.

Doubles teams should play to their strengths, with one player taking on more of the offensive shots while the other player taking on more of the defensive shots. This has the potential to produce a dynamic and productive approach for the team. Doubles teams can effectively cover the court and efficiently win points if they play to their strengths and capitalize on their advantages.

There are a number of significant distinctions to be made between singles and doubles pickleball. Players in a game of singles pickleball are responsible for covering the entire court on their own, whereas in a game of doubles pickleball, players cover the court by working together as a team. Because of the difference in court coverage, each game requires a different strategy as well as different shot placements.

Due to the fact that they are the only player responsible for scoring points, singles pickleball players are need to be more aggressive and focused on racking up points as rapidly as possible. When playing pickleball in a doubles match, players need to exercise greater patience and concentrate on setting up their partner for a winning shot.

The game of doubles pickleball needs an increased level of communication and coordination between partners, as they need to work together to cover the court and make it difficult for their opponents to return the ball. Players in singles pickleball are only able to rely on themselves and their own abilities and strategies in order to win games.

Chapter III

Basic Techniques

Grip and stance

Pickleball is a sport that players of all ages and ability levels can participate in and enjoy because it is both entertaining and fast-paced. To be successful in pickleball, you need a combination of physical and mental abilities, just as in any other sport; however, your grip and stance are two of the most significant components of the game.

The player's grip and stance are two of the most crucial components to master when learning how to play pickleball. They have a direct influence on how well you can move about the court, how much force you can create in your shots, and how well you can control the ball. The way in which you grip the paddle will have an effect on your stance, and vice versa. Grip and stance are very tightly tied to one another.

In pickleball, having a solid grip and stance will allow you to have greater control over the ball, which is one of the most important benefits of having a good grip and posture. If you have a solid grip, you'll be able to make more precise shots, and if you have a solid stance, you'll be able to move more quickly and smoothly around the court. You may be able to get an advantage over your competitors as a result of both of these aspects, and ultimately win the game as a result.

In the sport of pickleball, players have the option of utilizing a wide variety of grips, each of which comes with its own set of benefits and drawbacks. The continental grip, the eastern forehand grip, and the western forehand grip are the three varieties of grips that are used the most frequently.

The continental grip is the most adaptable sort of grip, and it is the one that players often use for all of the different types of strokes in pickleball. The thumb and index finger form a V shape as the paddle is held using this grip, with the base of the hand resting on the handle. This grip provides a good sense of control over the paddle, which is especially helpful while playing backhand shots.

The eastern forehand grip is quite similar to the continental forehand grip; the primary difference is that the base of the hand is positioned slightly toward the right side of the handle. This grip is perfect for playing forehand shots since it offers both control and power to the player.

A more extreme variation of the eastern forehand grip, the western forehand grip has the base of the hand pushed even further to the right side than it is in the eastern forehand grip. This grip is best suited for players who want to generate a lot of power in their forehand shots; however, it might be more challenging to maintain control with this grip.

In pickleball, there are a number of various stances that may be utilized, each of which has its own advantages and disadvantages based on the circumstances and the kind of shot that is being played. The ready stance, the forehand stance, and the backhand stance are the three varieties of stances that are used the most frequently.

The ready stance is the basic stance used in pickleball, and it requires standing with your feet shoulder-width apart and your knees slightly bent. This stance gives you the ability to move swiftly in any direction, making it an excellent choice for responding to the shots that your opponent takes.

The forehand stance is utilized when you are preparing to hit a forehand stroke, and it involves shifting your weight onto your left foot (for right-handed players) and taking a little step forward with your right foot. This stance is perfect for attacking shots since it enables you to produce more force in your forehand shots and is a good choice overall.

When you are getting ready to hit a backhand shot, you will utilize the backhand stance, which involves shifting your weight onto your right foot (for right-handed players) and taking a little step back with your left foot. This will allow you to hit the backhand shot more effectively. This stance lets you to create greater force in your backhand swings and is ideal for defense shots.

Personal preference can play a role in determining which grip and stance are best for your game; however, there are a few factors that should be taken into consideration before making a final choice.

First, consider your playing style. The continental grip and ready stance may be the optimal choice for you if you are a defensive player who relies on rapid reflexes and accurate shots. If you are an aggressive player who likes to attack the ball and produce power, you may find that the western forehand grip and the forehand stance are better ideal for you.

The second thing to think about is your physical capabilities. Because employing the western forehand grip might place additional strain on your wrist, you should probably avoid using it if you have a history of wrist or hand issues. This is because the grip can cause your wrist to twist awkwardly. If you have trouble moving around, you could find that having a wider stance, which helps with both balance and stability, is effective.

Finally, the best way to determine the appropriate grip and stance for your game is to practice and experiment with different combinations of the two. During your practice sessions, experiment with a variety of grips and stances to see which one feels the most natural to you and allows you to perform at your best.

Dinks and volleys

Pickleball is a sport that has gained more and more followers over the years as more and more people have been aware of how entertaining and exciting it can be to play. Players in any sport can improve their performance and gain an advantage over their opponents by employing a range of different techniques and strategies. Dinks and volleys are two of the most fundamental skills in the sport of pickleball. These techniques are vital for both the offensive and defensive play in the game.

Dinks and volleys are crucial skills in the sport of pickleball because they allow players to control the speed and direction of the ball, as well as provide opportunities for winning shots. Dinks and volleys also allow players to create more scoring opportunities. A dink is a short, soft shot that is hit just over the net and typically has a low trajectory. Dinks are most commonly employed in defensive strategies because they enable players to slow down the pace of the game and force their opponents to make mistakes.

On the other hand, volleys are shots that are hit before the ball bounces on the court, therefore they are called "before" shots. Players are able to keep control of the ball and keep the pressure on their opponents when they employ volley balls, which can be used in both offensive and defensive play.

Players need to be able to make accurate shots while maintaining a high degree of control in order to be successful at dinks and volleys. Both of these shot types involve a great level of ability and precision. They also need great footwork and positioning, as players need to be in the ideal position to make the shot and move fast to get into position for the next shot.

Dinking requires players to have a good touch and solid control over the ball in order for it to be successful. The key to a successful dink is to hit the ball gently and with a low trajectory so that it goes over the net and settles on the opponent's court at the very edge of the opponents court. The ball is usually hit with an upward swing, and the paddle is used to lift the ball up and over the net. This shot is called a dink.

When hitting a dink, it is essential to have in mind to keep the ball at a low trajectory relative to the ground as this is one of the most significant considerations. When taking the shot, you can do this by keeping the paddle at a low angle and in close proximity to the net. Players should also try to aim towards the corners of their opponent's court, since this can make it more difficult for the opponent to return the shot to the player's court.

Players need to have excellent hand-eye coordination as well as quick reflexes in order to execute a successful volley. Players are able to keep control of the ball and sustain pressure on their opponents when they successfully make contact with the ball before it bounces on the court. This is the key to a solid volley and the most effective way to do it.

Players should make every effort to keep their paddle in front of them and their body oriented toward the net while they are hitting a volley. They are able to respond rapidly to the ball and take an accurate shot as a result of this. There are several different grips that can be used to hit volley, including the continental grip, the eastern forehand grip, and the western forehand grip.

When you hit a volley, it's essential to make sure that the ball stays low to the ground. This is one of the most important things to keep in mind. This can be performed by striking the ball with a motion that is slightly downward, while hitting the ball towards the direction of the opponent's court with the paddle. Players should also try to aim towards the corners of their opponent's court, since this can make it more difficult for the opponent to return the shot to the player's court.

Dinks and volleys are two essential methods in pickleball, and if you work them into your overall game strategy, you can give yourself an advantage over your opponents and make the game more enjoyable for yourself. Dinks and volleys are great additions to any game, and here are some pointers on how to include them:

Dinks and volleys are two fundamental skills that are essential to acquire if you want to be successful at the sport of pickleball. However, relying just on these strategies is not sufficient to ensure victory in the game. A player needs to become proficient at switching up their shots and incorporating these changes into their overall game plan. This means that they should change the speed and trajectory of their strokes so that their opponents are unable to predict what they are going to do next. For instance, a player can hit a low dink followed by a hard volley or a high lob followed by a low dink.

Dinks are especially helpful for defensive play since they have the ability to slow down the action of the game and push the other team to make mistakes. When players are under pressure or when their opponent is at the net, they should employ dinks to give themselves some time to get back into position and reclaim control of the point.

On the other side, volleys are fantastic for offensive play and should be used whenever possible. Players are able to maintain pressure on their opponents and create possibilities for winning shots through the use of these techniques. Players should make advantage of volleys when they are close to the net and have the opportunity to put the ball away. Volleys are particularly effective in these situations.

In addition to being proficient in the skills of dinks and volleys, players also need to concentrate on improving their footwork and positioning. Dinks and volleys require players to have excellent footwork and positioning in order to be successful. Players also need to be able to move around the court quickly and effectively in order to maintain their position and to make the shot. Drills that concentrate on footwork and positioning, such as the figure eight drill or the around the world drill, should be practiced often.

Finally, it is imperative to select the appropriate grip and stance in order to successfully perform dinks and volleys. Players are required to choose a grip and stance that not only seem natural to them but also enable them to make precise shots while maintaining a high level of control. During practice, it might be helpful for players to try out a variety of different grips and stances in order to determine which ones are most advantageous for them.

Forehand and backhand strokes

Players in the sport of pickleball need to have a diverse set of talents in order to compete successfully. These skills include good footwork, quick reflexes, and accurate shots. Pickleball is a fun and fast-paced sport. The forehand and backhand strokes are two of the most significant shots in pickleball. These strokes are critical for both offensive and defensive play in the game.

Both the forehand and backhand strokes are considered to be two of the most essential shots in pickleball due to the fact that they enable players to control the speed and trajectory of the ball. The forehand stroke is a shot that is hit with the paddle on the same side as the player's dominant hand, whereas the backhand stroke is a shot that is hit with the paddle on the opposite side of the player's dominant hand.

Because they need players to be able to make accurate shots while maintaining a high degree of control, the forehand and backhand strokes both require a great level of skill and precision from their users. They also need excellent footwork and positioning, as players need to be in the ideal position to make the shot and move fast to get into position for the next shot.

Players need to have strong hand-eye coordination and a firm hold on the paddle in order to perform an effective forehand stroke. The secret to a powerful forehand stroke is to keep the paddle perpendicular to the ground at all times and to make a fluid motion with your arms as you move it from the back to the front of the court. Players should make it their goal to strike the ball in the center of their paddles and use a slight upward motion when doing so to assist in lifting the ball over the net.

Players need to have sufficient wrist flexibility and a solid hold on the paddle in order to execute an effective backhand stroke in the game. The secret to a powerful backhand stroke is to keep the paddle perpendicular to the ground at all times and to make a smooth motion with your arms as you move it from the back to the front of the court. Players should make it their goal to strike the ball in the middle of the paddle and do so with a slight downward motion, as this will help keep the ball at a manageable height and make it easier to keep under control.

It is crucial to remember to follow through with the swing when playing both forehand and backhand strokes, as this is one of the most critical things you can do. This implies prolonging the action of the swing after making contact with the ball, which can help add more force to the shot while also giving the player more control over it.

The forehand and backhand strokes are both essential strategies in the sport of pickleball. Incorporating these strokes into your overall game plan will help you get a competitive advantage over your opponents. The following are some pointers that can help you improve your game by incorporating forehand and backhand strokes:

When using forehand and backhand strokes, one of the most essential considerations to keep in mind is to switch up your shots from time to time. This involves striking the ball in a variety of ways, including with varying speeds, trajectories, and spins, so that your opponents are unable to predict what moves you will make next. For instance, you could begin by hitting a strong forehand followed by a backhand that is spinning and gentle.

Because it enables players to generate force and put the ball away, the forehand stroke is extremely useful for offensive play. When you have a good chance of hitting a winner with your forehand shot or when you want to force your opponent onto the defensive, use this shot.

The backhand stroke is very useful for defensive play because it enables players to keep the ball low and under control. This makes the backhand stroke highly effective. You should try to hit backhand shots when you are under pressure or when your opponent is at the net, as this can give you some time to get back into position and reclaim control of the point.

Both the forehand and backhand strokes require good footwork and positioning in order to be successful. You need to make sure that you are in the ideal position to make the shot, and that you are moving about the court in a quick and effective manner. The three-point exercise and the diagonal movement drill are two examples of the types of drills that should be practiced in order to improve footwork and positioning.

Your ability to execute forehand and backhand strokes successfully can be greatly influenced by the grip you use and the stance you have when playing the game. You should select a grip and stance that both feel natural to you and enable you to make precise shots while maintaining a high degree of control. During your practice sessions, try out a variety of different grips and stances until you discover the ones that are most effective for you.

Overhead smashes

In recent years, pickleball has emerged as a competitive sport with a reputation for being both fast-paced and thrilling. It's a combination sport that incorporates aspects of badminton, ping pong, and tennis, and it's played on a court that's roughly a third of the size of a regular tennis court. The overhead smash is a powerful stroke that can be utilized in pickleball to put away points and intimidate opponents. It is often considered to be one of the most exciting shots in the game.

To begin, let's take a more in-depth look at the overhead smash and what it actually entails. It basically consists of a powerful shot that is hit from above the head, usually while the player is at or close to the net. The overhead smash is often utilized as a response to a high ball that has been thrown by the opponent or as a follow-up to a weak return that has left the court open for a powerful attack.

The player must first get themself into the appropriate position in order to successfully execute an overhead smash. They should be facing the net while standing with their feet about shoulder-width apart, gripping the paddle with both hands. Because this shot is most successful when it is hit from a close range, the player should also be positioned near the net.

The next step is for the player to get ready to hit the ball. This is accomplished by bringing the paddle back behind the head while bending the elbows and ensuring that a comfortable grasp is maintained on the paddle with the hands. When the ball is getting closer, the player needs to take a step forward with the foot that is leading, then shift their weight to the foot that remains behind while they swing the paddle forward.

The swing itself should be a smooth, fluid motion that begins behind the head and ends with the paddle striking the ball at the highest position possible. When the player wants to generate power, they should rotate their hips and shoulders as they swing the paddle forward. The objective is to make it difficult for the opponent to return the shot by striking the ball with sufficient force to send it deep into the opponent's court.

Of course, pulling off an overhead smash is easier said than done. It is important to keep in mind a few essential aspects if you want this shot to be as successful as possible. To begin, it is essential to keep a tight eye on the ball and ensure that the swing is perfectly timed. This means you should hold off on swinging the paddle forward until the ball has reached its highest point before you do so. If the player swings too early or too late, they will either entirely miss the ball or hit a weak shot that is simple for the other player to return.

The angle at which the paddle is held is also a significant consideration. When trying to execute an overhead smash, the player should focus on making contact with the ball with the paddle's edge rather than the face of the paddle. This helps in producing topspin on the ball, which makes it more challenging for the opponent to return the ball. It is also essential to keep the paddle level during the swing, rather than angling it up or down, as doing so will throw off the shot's trajectory and cause it to head off in the wrong direction.

Therefore, under what circumstances does it make sense to execute an overhead smash when playing pickleball? As was indicated before, this shot is generally performed in response to a high ball or a weak return from the opponent. On the other hand, it is essential to make strategic use of the overhead smash rather than simply relying on hitting it every time the opportunity presents itself. A low, quick shot that bounces quickly and prevents the opponent from having time to react, for instance, may be more effective if the opponent is standing far away from the net. In the same manner, if your opponent is anticipating an overhead smash from you, it is probably best to switch things up and hit a drop shot or a cross-court shot instead of the one they are expecting.

Chapter IV

Strategy and Tactics

Basic strategies for singles and doubles play

The past few years have seen a rise in participation in the sport of pickleball, which is a lot of fun and very exciting. It is a sport that incorporates aspects of tennis, badminton, and ping pong, and it can be played either as a singles or a doubles competition. There are a few fundamental methods that can be of assistance to players on the court, regardless of whether they are competing alone or with a partner.

Let's begin by taking a look at some fundamental methods for playing singles first. When playing singles, the court is significantly smaller than when playing doubles, and there is only one opponent for each player to contend with. As a result, in order to score points, players need to employ strategy and make the most of the opportunities presented to them.

When playing singles, it's crucial to remember to keep the ball in play as much as possible. Although it might not appear to be very effective at first, it really is pretty powerful. Players may bring their opponents down and push them to make mistakes by engaging in a back-and-forth exchange with the ball with their opponent. It's not as vital to strive to smash the ball as hard as you can; rather, it's important to aim for consistency and precision with each stroke you take.

The ability to maintain patience is another essential tactic for singles. It's tempting to let frustration get the best of you and try to force a shot, but doing so typically results in missed opportunities and wasted points. Instead, players should concentrate on maintaining the ball in play and looking for opportunities to attack when they present themselves. This could mean waiting for the opponent to make a mistake in their return, or it could mean setting up a shot with a succession of volleys that are well-placed.

When it comes to attacking, there are few kinds of essential shots that are especially useful in singles competition. The first stroke is called a drop shot, and it is a gentle shot that is meant to land just over the net. This causes the opponent to have to move forward in order to receive the ball. After this, a lob, which is a high shot that lands deep in the opponent's court and gives the player time to get back into position, can be executed as a follow-up move. The overhead smash is the third stroke in this sequence. It is a strong shot that can be utilized to put the ball away and win the point.

Now that we have everything out of the way, let's have a look at some fundamental methods for playing doubles. When playing doubles, the court is longer and wider, and there are two more players to contend with. This indicates that in order for players to be successful, they need to collaborate and communicate effectively with one another.

When playing doubles, establishing a strong position at the net is a vital part of your game strategy. This means getting onto the net as quickly as possible and remaining on it for as long as possible. Players have the ability of taking control of the point and force their opponents to take shots that are more difficult to accomplish when they do this.

When playing doubles, one of the most crucial strategies is to communicate clearly and effectively with one's partner. This entails not only keeping track of your own movements but also calling out shots and positions to your opponent. Players are able to cover more ground and make it more difficult for their opponents to hit wins when they cooperate as a team and work together.

There are a few of essential strokes that should be kept in mind when attempting to attack in doubles play. The first stroke is called a dink and it is a gentle shot that is hit just over the net and landing in the kitchen of the opponent (which is the area that is close to the net). This shot can be used to build up a powerful groundstroke or overhead smash, which can be hit by either player.

The cross-court shot is another effective shot that may be used in doubles play. This strategy is striking the ball in such a way that it travels diagonally across the court, making it more difficult for the adversaries to track down. This shot has the potential to break down defensive positions and open up scoring possibilities for the other team.

Last but not least, the lob can be an effective shot when playing doubles. This shot can be utilized to gain an advantage by stalling time and creating opportunities to get closer to the goal. Additionally, it can be utilized to push the opponents back, thereby opening up room for the player to move forward.

When playing doubles, it is essential to bear in mind not just these particular shots but also certain basic techniques as well. When developing a plan, it is crucial to remember to avoid hitting the ball through the middle of the court because doing so provides an easy opportunity for the other team to attack. Players should instead focus on hitting the ball to the sidelines, as this makes it harder for their opponents to hit wins.

In doubles play, switching sides with one's partner regularly is an additional crucial approach that should be utilized. This helps to keep the opponent guessing, and it also prevents them from becoming too comfortable with one particular pattern of play. Additionally, it enables every player to play to their individual strengths while simultaneously covering more distance on the field.

These tactics are, of course, merely the beginning of the process. When playing singles or doubles, there are a variety of other considerations that can come into play, such as court positioning, shot selection, and mental concentration, among others. The goal is to maintain flexibility and adaptability, and be willing to modify one's strategy as necessary based on the circumstances at hand.

How to play against different opponents

Pickleball is a sport that can be enjoyed by people of many ages and levels of expertise, making it a sport that is both entertaining and thrilling. It is a game that involves strategy as well as the ability to modify one's playing style to match the strengths and weaknesses of one's opponents in order to win.

When playing pickleball, you can go up against an opponent who is known as an aggressive player. Someone like this likes to hit strong shots and take early control of the point when it's available to them. It can be difficult to compete while playing against an opponent that is aggressive, but there are several methods that can assist you.

The first thing you need to do while playing against opponents who are aggressive is to get familiar with their playing style. Players that play aggressively typically hit their shots with more force and take early control of the point. They could also aim to create errors by shooting shots that are difficult for the other team to return. Once you have a grasp of their playing style, you will be able to predict their shots and be ready to respond to them.

Playing defense against opponents that like to be aggressive is one of the most effective techniques in competitive sports. This indicates that you should stop trying to hit the ball and instead concentrate on keeping the ball in play. You can force your opponent to make more mistakes and hit more shots if you play defensively and compel them to hit more shots. This can also help to slow down the speed of the game, giving you greater control over the point you're playing for.

Soft shots, such as drop shots and dinks, are another approach that can be utilized for great benefit while playing against opponents that are aggressive. These shots have the potential to disrupt the rhythm of offensive players, so making it more difficult for those players to attack. As a result of the sudden change in pace, aggressive players may be caught off guard and unable to score points after being presented with opportunities created by soft shots.

When playing against opponents who are aggressive, it can be difficult, but it's crucial to keep a strong mentality and not let yourself become discouraged. You have a better chance of succeeding if you don't let frustration get the best of you and have a positive attitude, even though it's easy to become frustrated and make mistakes. This also involves avoiding taking risks that aren't essential and not acting in an overly aggressive manner yourself.

Players that play aggressively have a greater tendency to take control of the point by making shots down the center of the court. It is important that you keep the ball away from the middle of the court and instead go for the sidelines in order to successfully combat this. Because of this, it may become more difficult for aggressive players to attack, and it may also provide you with opportunities to hit wins.

When playing against opponents that are aggressive, it is essential to keep your patience and refrain from trying to force shots. If you are patient and wait for the appropriate opportunity, you will be able to take control of the point and win the game. Aggressive players could try to cause errors by hitting shots that are difficult to return, but if you are patient, you can take control of the point and win the game.

Altering your playing style in response to an aggressive opponent is another method that has proven to be successful. This involves using a number of different shots, such as lobs and drop shots, to maintain your opponent's level of confusion. You can generate openings and opportunities to hit wins by varying the shots that you take in the game.

It is crucial to maintain a positive attitude and have confidence in one's abilities even when competing against opponents who are aggressive. This includes keeping your concentration on your game plan even when things aren't going the way you want them to and not allowing yourself to become discouraged. It also involves maintaining self-assurance in your skills and not being hesitant to take chances when the situation calls for it.

When playing pickleball, you could also go up against a player that plays defense. This is yet another type of opponent. Someone like this prefers to play a lot of dinks and delicate shots, and they could be reluctant to take risks. When playing against an opponent who is defensive, you need to be patient and strategic.

The first thing you need to do while playing against opponents who play defensively is to get familiar with their playing style. Players that play defense have a tendency to play a lot of dinks and soft shots, and they are sometimes hesitant to take risks. They could also be patient, waiting for their opponent to make a mistake in order to capitalize on the opportunity. Once you have a grasp of their playing style, you will be able to predict their shots and be ready to respond to them.

When playing against opponents who like to play defense, one of the most effective methods is to play in an aggressive manner. This involves taking control of the point at an early stage and hitting difficult shots in order to force the defensive player into the back foot. They will be forced out of their comfort zone, which will increase the likelihood that they will make mistakes as a result of your actions.

Utilizing a wide variety of shot types is one of the most successful strategies to adopt when going up against opponents who play defense. This means that you should utilize a variety of shots, like as drop shots, lobs, and other shots, in order to keep the defensive player guessing about your next move. You will be able to create openings and possibilities to hit wins if you act in this manner.

It is important to have patience and refrain from trying to force shots when competing against opponents that take a defensive approach to the game. You may have to wait longer to earn points, but if you maintain your concentration and play intelligently, you can still come out on top. This entails waiting for the right moment to make a winning shot rather than attempting to force a shot and make mistake.

When playing against opponents who are defensive, it can be difficult, but it's crucial to keep a strong mentality and not let yourself become disheartened. You have a better chance of succeeding if you don't let frustration get the best of you and have a positive attitude, even though it's easy to become frustrated and make mistakes. This involves avoiding taking risks that aren't essential and not acting in an overly aggressive manner yourself.

Maintaining your usual level of play is another useful tactic to employ when facing opponents that favor a defensive stance. Instead of focusing on hitting winners, this strategy calls for hitting shots that are high and deep. If you do this, you may force the defensive player to attempt more shots, which will in turn cause them to make more errors. It also means avoiding making unforced errors, like hitting the ball out of bounds or into the net.

When playing defense, it's common for players to take a number of dinks and other easy shots, which can make it challenging to get into a rhythm. It is essential to be ready to move around and cover a significant amount of ground in order to combat this. Being able to predict where the ball will go as well as having good footwork and quick reflexes are all necessary for this.

As a result of the increased degree of control it offers them over the play, defensive players like taking shots that are directed toward the court's center. It is important that you keep the ball away from the middle of the court and instead go for the sidelines in order to successfully combat this. This can make it more difficult for defensive players to attack, which opens the door for you to hit winners and gives you additional opportunities.

The quick player is a third sort of opponent that you could face when playing pickleball. This refers to a player that is quick and agile, and who has the potential to get to shots that other players are unable to. Strategy and awareness are both required while playing against an opponent who is quick.

The first thing you need to do while playing against opponents that are quick is to get a feel for their playing style. Players who are quick are typically agile and fast, and they may be able to get to shots that other players are unable to. It's also possible that they're more at ease performing at a faster pace. Once you have a grasp of their playing style, you will be able to predict their actions and be ready to respond to them.

When playing against opponents that are speedy, aiming towards the sidelines is one of the most effective methods you can do. This entails striking shots that are aimed at the four corners of the court, as opposed to hitting shots that are intended directly at the opponent. You can push your opponent to cover more ground by doing this, which in turn may give you more opportunity to strike winners and increase your winning percentage.

The utilization of drop shots and lobs is another approach that proves to be successful while playing against opponents who are speedy. It is possible to slow down the pace of the game by using drop shots, which also makes it more challenging for players who are quick to get to the ball. It is possible to take advantage of a quick opponent's speed and tire them out by using lobs.

To successfully combat the movements of quick opponents, you need to have excellent footwork and fast reactions. It is essential to be ready to move around and cover a significant amount of ground in order to combat this. This requires you to maintain a state of greater awareness and be prepared to move in any given direction. In addition to this, it involves being ready to hit shots from a variety of various places on the court.

When playing against opponents that are quick, it's important to try and anticipate their actions. This is an effective tactic. This requires keeping track of their footwork and figuring out where they will be on the court before they get there. When you do this, you put yourself in a position to hit shots that your opponent might not be expecting you to hit.

When competing against opponents that are quick, maintaining consistency is of the utmost importance. Instead of focusing on hitting winners, this strategy calls for shooting shots that are high and deep. You can force your opponent to hit more shots and make more mistakes if you do this to them. It also means avoiding making unforced errors, like hitting the ball out of bounds or into the net.

When playing against opponents that are quick, it can be difficult, but it's important to keep a strong mentality and not let yourself get disheartened. You have a better chance of succeeding if you don't let frustration get the best of you and have a positive attitude, even though it's easy to become frustrated and make mistakes. This involves avoiding taking risks that aren't essential and not acting in an overly aggressive manner yourself.

Changing the shots you take is a further method that can be used to effectively compete against quick opponents. This entails employing a number of different shots, such as lobs and drop shots, to maintain your opponent's level of confusion. You can generate openings and opportunities to hit winners by varying the shots that you take in the game.

In pickleball, it's possible that some of your opponents won't have much experience. These players are fresh to the sport and may not yet have acquired strong abilities or strategy. They are referred to as "novices." When playing against an opponent with less experience, you need to show patience and kindness.

When competing against opponents with a lack of experience, it is essential to show patience and refrain from taking advantage of their weaknesses. This means avoiding strokes that may be too difficult for them to return, and being patient with them when they make mistakes in their play. Your opponent will be able to enhance their skills and have a better time playing the game if you do this for them.

When playing against opponents who lack expertise, one useful technique is to offer advice and pointers to assist them improve their game. This entails not only being patient with them when they make mistakes but also offering guidance on how they can improve their shots and strategies. Your opponent will be able to enhance their skills and have a better time playing the game if you do this for them.

The use of a partner is an efficient strategy that can be utilized while playing against opponents that lack prior experience. This entails playing doubles with an experienced player and a less skilled player on each of the two teams. This allows the more experienced player to provide the less experienced player with assistance and support, which in turn helps the less experienced player develop their skills and enjoy the game more.

When playing against opponents that lack experience, it is essential to keep your concentration on keeping the ball in play. This means avoiding shots that are too difficult for them to return and hitting shots that are aimed towards the middle of the court rather than the sidelines or the net. Your opponent will be able to enhance their skills and have a better time playing the game if you do this for them.

When playing against opponents that lack expertise, it is important not to overwhelm them as this is another effective technique. This requires not hitting shots that are too quick or too difficult for them to return, as well as having patience when they do make errors in their play. Your opponent will be able to enhance their skills and have a better time playing the game if you do this for them.

When playing against opponents with less experience than you, it might be difficult, but it's crucial to keep their spirits up and do what you can to make sure they enjoy the game. This entails complimenting them on their efforts and standing by them when they make mistakes by providing support. Your opponent will be able to enhance their skills and have a better time playing the game if you do this for them.

When competing against opponents with a lack of expertise, it is essential to show proper courtesy and refrain from taking advantage of their shortcomings. This means avoiding strokes that may be too difficult for them to return, and being patient with them when they make mistakes in their play. Your opponent will be able to enhance their skills and have a better time playing the game if you do this for them.

Tips for improving your game

Pickleball is a sport that combines agility, strategy, and skill, and it moves at a fast pace, making it a very entertaining and competitive activity. There are always new methods to enhance your game and take it to the next level, no matter how long you've been playing or how much experience you already have.

Regular practice is the first and most important piece of advice for developing your pickleball game. Practice as much as you can. This requires you to set aside time, both on and off the court, to hone your skills in terms of hitting and technique. The more you practice, the better you will get, and the more secure you will feel when you go to the court.

When you're working on your serve, return, volley, and footwork in practice, it's essential to split your attention between all of these aspects of the game. You should practice a variety of strokes, such as drop shots, dinks, and overheads, and you should also practice hitting those shots from a variety of various places on the court. You can also practice with a partner by engaging in drills and games that place an emphasis on particular abilities and techniques.

A player needs to have excellent footwork in order to have the ability to hit shots from a variety of positions and angles, as well as to respond fast to the shots that their opponent hits. Focus on developing quick reflexes and solid balance, as well as the ability to move quickly and smoothly across the court, to improve your footwork.

Ladder drills are an excellent activity to participate in if you want to enhance your footwork. During these exercises, a ladder is set up on the court, and the participant is required to run through it at varying speeds and in a variety of directions. Your agility, foot speed, and overall coordination will all likely increase as a result of this.

Pickleball's serve is one of the game's most crucial shots, and working on your serve may have a significant impact on how well you play overall. This requires practice with a variety of serves, such as the lob serve, the drive serve, and the drop serve, as well as the ability to position the ball in a variety of locations across the court.

In order to enhance your serve, you must pay special attention to your throw as well as your technique. Make sure that your throw is consistent and in the appropriate position, and work on giving the ball the appropriate amount of spin and power when you hit it.

The volley is another essential shot in pickleball, and working on your volley technique can have a significant impact for the rest of your game. This involves perfecting your technique, such as being able to maintain your paddle elevated and strike the ball with accuracy and control through repeated practice.

Using a wall as a target for your practice might be an efficient approach to enhance your volley. While standing somewhat near to the wall, practice your technique and footwork by repeatedly hitting the ball back and forth. In addition, you can practice volleys with a partner, striking the ball back and forth at varying speeds and angles.

Pickleball is a game of strategy, and if you want to take your game to the next level, developing your strategy is one of the most important things you can do. This requires you to devise a strategy for each individual point, as well as the ability to modify that approach in response to the strengths and weaknesses presented by your opponent.

It is essential to familiarize yourself with the game and become familiar with the various strategies, techniques, and approaches that are available. Observe and examine the methods and strategies employed by professional players, and pay attention to both your own abilities and those of the players you watch. This can help you establish a solid strategy that can assist you in taking control of the point and increasing the likelihood of you coming out on top overall.

Playing with a variety of people can help you improve in a variety of different aspects of your game. When you compete against other players who have more experience than you have, you have the opportunity to pick up new skills and methods. You will be able to enhance your consistency and timing if you compete against other players who have a skill level comparable to your own. And if you play with players who have less experience than you do, not only will you have the opportunity to hone your own hitting and technical skills, but you will also be able to assist those players in developing their abilities.

You may enhance your overall game by playing with a variety of people since this will help you get a better understanding of the various playing styles and techniques that are used by other players. So, whether it's in a league, a tournament, or simply a casual game with friends, you should make an effort to compete against a variety of different players as much as you can.

Observing and gaining knowledge from the play of other pickleball players is one of the most efficient ways to improve your own game. This requires not only watching top players and learning from their plans and techniques, but also reviewing your own matches and evaluating your own capabilities and determining where you need improvement.

When you watch professional players, you should focus on their footwork, shot selection, serve, return, and strategy. Pay attention to how they move their feet. You should make an effort to include these aspects in your own game and practice playing with them on the court.

When you view replays of your own matches, pay close attention to areas in which you may make progress toward becoming a better player, including as your footwork, shot selection, and overall strategy. This can assist you in determining the areas of your game in which you need to concentrate your training and will ultimately help you become a better player over time.

In conclusion, it is essential to maintain a positive mindset while concentrating on getting better at your game. This means that you should not allow yourself to become discouraged when you make mistakes, nor should you allow yourself to become overconfident when you are playing well.

Pickleball is a sport that needs mental toughness, and maintaining a positive attitude which can help you in maintaining motivation and staying focused on your objectives. Therefore, you should always make an effort to have a positive attitude and remain focused on improving your performance, and you should keep in mind that even the top players have potential for improvement.

Chapter V

Fitness and Training

Warm-up and stretching exercises

The sport of pickleball, which is played at a fast pace and places a high demand on one's physical fitness, calls for a combination of strength, agility, and endurance. It is crucial to properly warm up before playing, and to include stretching exercises as a regular part of your practice, in order to reduce the risk of injury and improve overall performance.

Before we get into particular exercises, let's talk about how important it is to warm up and stretch before playing a game of pickleball.

The increase blood flow to your muscles that results from warming up is one of the ways that you may get them ready for exercise. Additionally, it helps to enhance both your heart rate and your respiratory rate, both of which can contribute to an improvement in your overall performance as well as a reduction in the chance of injury. If you correctly warm up, you may enhance both your reaction time and your mental attention, which will allow you to play more effectively and improve your overall performance.

Exercises that focus on stretching are also essential for reducing the risk of injury and maximizing performance. The act of stretching can assist to increase your flexibility and range of motion, both of which can make it easier for you to move around the court and lower the likelihood that you will get an injury. Stretching can help minimize muscle pain and exhaustion, allowing you to play for longer and recover more quickly.

In order to participate in any kind of sport in a way that is both safe and effective, it is necessary to get your body ready for the activity. Warming up before playing any sport, including pickleball, is vital to lower the chance of injury and increase performance when you're out of the court. The following are some examples of warm-up activities that can assist you in getting ready to play pickleball:

Jogging or walking quickly at a brisk pace is the first warm-up activity that you can try. Jogging or walking quickly for five to ten minutes will get your heart rate up and boost the amount of blood that is pumped to your muscles. This is an excellent workout for getting your whole body ready for action and warming it up before you start.

After that, move on to high knees. While running in place or moving ahead, bring your knees as high as you can towards your chest and lift them as much as you can. This workout will help you warm up your hip flexors, quads, and core, all of which are important muscle groups to have if you want to be successful at playing pickleball.

Butt kicks are another effective workout that you may use to warm up. While you are running in place or moving ahead, bring your heels up near your buttocks and kick them. This exercise serves to warm up your hamstrings and glutes, which are important for movements on the court such as jumping and lunging.

Warming up your muscles with side shuffles is another fantastic way to do it. Side-to-side shuffle while maintaining a forward-pointing stance with your feet and a slight bend in your knees. Warming up your hip adductors and abductors, which are essential for making lateral movements on the court, is facilitated by this exercise.

Last but not least, lunges are a great exercise to use as a warm-up for your lower body. Take a big steps forward with one foot while maintaining a straight spine and ensuring that your knee is higher than your ankle. First bring your back knee closer to the ground, and then immediately push yourself back up. This exercise serves to warm up your quads, hamstrings, and glutes, all of which are crucial for movements on the court such as jumping, lunging, and pivoting.

Pickleball is just like any other sport because it requires you to stretch before and after each game. Stretching is an essential component of any workout program. When playing pickleball, stretching properly can help improve your flexibility, reduce muscle pain and fatigue, and lower the likelihood that you will get an injury. When playing pickleball, the following stretching exercises will help increase your flexibility, hence reducing the likelihood that you will get an injury:

The quad stretch is the first stretching exercise that you will perform. Maintain a hip-width distance between your feet as you stand and bring one heel toward your buttocks. Keep one hand on your ankle while you use the other to move your heel toward your buttocks in a gentle manner. After holding this position for thirty seconds, switch sides. Your quadriceps will become more flexible as a result of this stretch, which is beneficial for activities like jumping and lunging.

Try out the hamstring stretch after that. Take a seat on the ground with your legs extended in front of you in a straight line. Maintain a straight back while you bring your hands closer to your feet and try to touch your toes. Maintain this hold for thirty seconds. Hamstring flexibility is essential for performing a variety of motions, including reaching and lunging, and this stretch will help you achieve it.

In order to get your upper body ready for pickleball, shoulder stretches are another essential component. Place your feet approximately hip-width apart and bring one arm across your chest while standing. Make use of the opposite arm to give your arm a little pull in the direction of your chest. After holding this position for thirty seconds, switch sides. Shoulders and upper back can become more flexible with the help of this stretch.

When it comes to lowering the possibility of being hurt while playing pickleball, calf stretches can be very helpful. Position yourself so that you are facing a wall with your hands on the wall and one foot behind you. Maintain the straight position of your back leg and keep your heel on the ground. Lean forward until you feel a stretch in your calf. Continue doing this until you reach the wall. After holding this position for thirty seconds, switch sides.

Another essential stretching exercise for pickleball players is the hip flexor stretch. Get down on your knees and position your feet so that one is in front of you and the other is behind you. Keep your back in a neutral position and press your hips forward in a controlled manner until you feel a stretch in the front of your hips. After holding this position for thirty seconds, turn sides. This stretch can help loosen up your hip flexors, which are essential for activities like running and lunging.

Stretching your side muscles and obliques with the side stretch is another helpful workout that can help you achieve greater flexibility. Place your feet approximately hip-width apart and stretch one arm up towards the ceiling while standing. While keeping your feet firmly planted on the ground, bend your arm at the elbow and lean your body to the opposite side. After holding this position for thirty seconds, switch sides.

The wrist stretch has the potential to be beneficial for both your wrists and your forearms. You should be standing with your arm extended in front of you with the palm facing downward. Make use of your other hand to give your fingers a slight stretch by drawing them in the direction of your wrist until you feel it in your forearm. After holding this position for thirty seconds, switch sides.

Finally, remember to stretch your neck muscles to lessen the likelihood of experiencing pain or stiffness in your neck. Place yourself in a seated position on the floor with your legs crossed, and then turn your head to one side. To stretch your neck, use your hand to pull your head towards your shoulder in a gentle manner until you feel a stretch in your neck. After holding this position for thirty seconds, switch sides.

Now that you have some stretches and warm-up exercises to do, I'll give you some pointers on how to incorporate them into your pickleball routine:

When you are initially beginning with warm-up and stretching activities, it is essential to get started slowly in order to avoid injuring yourself. Be careful not to overexert yourself, and as you become used to the routine, gradually build up the intensity of your workouts as well as the length of time you spend doing them. This will assist you in avoiding injury and will guarantee that you are well prepared for each of your games.

It is essential that you do not overlook these exercises, regardless of whether you are pressed for time or ready to get started playing the game. If you skip warm-up and stretching activities, you expose yourself to a greater risk of injury and may have a more difficult time performing on the court. In order to ensure that you are well prepared for each game, you need make them a priority in your routine.

It is important that you pay attention to your body and react accordingly while you are warming up and stretching. Pay attention to how each activity makes your body feel, and if something doesn't seem right or if you're feeling discomfort, stop the exercise and consult a coach or a medical practitioner for guidance. This will help you avoid injury and ensure that you are appropriately preparing your body for the physical activities that you have planned.

It can be difficult to incorporate warm-up and stretching activities into your routine, but it's important to make them a consistent component of your pickleball practice routine. Because of this, you will be able to cultivate healthy habits and guarantee that you are preparing your body well for each game. Find a schedule that suits you well and commit to sticking with it.

Finally, it is really necessary that you drink enough of water while you are warming up and stretching. It is important to consume a large amount of water before, during, and after your workouts in order to reduce the risk of cramping and enhance your overall performance.

Conditioning and strength training

Pickleball is a well-liked sport that can be played successfully by players of varying ages and degrees of expertise. Combining elements of tennis, badminton, and ping pong, this sport is played on a court that is roughly the same size as a court designed for playing doubles badminton. The ball used in the game is a little one made of perforated plastic, and the paddles used are about the same size as those used in ping pong. The objective of the game is to knock the ball over the net and have it to land inside the court of the other team without the opposition team being able to successfully return the ball to their own court. The game calls for a combination of speed, agility, endurance, and strength; hence, it is essential for players to have sufficient conditioning and strength training in order to compete successfully.

Pickleball is a sport that demands players to exert a significant amount of physical effort and to move fast around the court. Depending on the skill level of the players and the format of the game that is being played, the length of time that is spent playing can range anywhere from a few minutes to many hours. Players can enhance their endurance by engaging in appropriate conditioning and strength training, which enables them to play for longer periods of time during games and at a higher level overall. Running, cycling, and swimming are all examples of activities that fall under the category of cardiovascular exercise. These activities can assist athletes increase their cardiovascular capacity and endurance. Players should strive to engage in cardiovascular exercise for at least thirty to sixty minutes, three to five times each week.

Pickleball is a sport that requires players to be able to move rapidly and change directions at a moment's notice, therefore speed and agility are two qualities that are essential to the sport. Conditioning and strength training done correctly can help develop these abilities, making it possible for players to move around the court at a faster and more efficient pace. A player's speed and agility on the court can be improved by the use of agility drills including as the ladder drill, the cone drill, and the jumping drill. The explosiveness and quickness of a player can also be improved through the use of plyometric exercises. Some examples of these exercises include jumping lunges and box jumps. Players should strive to include agility drills and plyometric exercises in their strength training and conditioning routine two to three times per week at the very least.

Pickleball, like many other sports, has a high incidence of injuries. However, appropriate strength training and conditioning can help prevent injuries by boosting overall fitness levels, as well as strengthening muscles, improving flexibility, and expanding range of motion in the joints. Exercises that focus on resistance training, such as lunges, squats, and push-ups, can help important muscular areas, such as the legs, core, and upper body, improve strength and endurance. Because it assists in the improvement of flexibility and aids in the prevention of injury, stretching is an essential component of any program designed to condition the body and build muscle. Pickleball players should stretch before and after each game, as well as on days when there are no matches scheduled. A player's total fitness program could benefit from including yoga and pilates, which are both good types of stretching and can be practiced anywhere.

Conditioning and strength training can assist players improve their overall performance in pickleball by enhancing their endurance, speed, agility, and strength. This may result in increased victories, advancements in ranks, and an increased level of enjoyment from the sport. The goal of players should be to perform resistance training two to three times a week, with each session focused on a different muscle group. They should also make it a priority to include aerobic exercise, drills that focus on agility, and stretching as part of their overall routine of strength training and conditioning.

Pickleball players who want to enhance their game should build a comprehensive conditioning and strength training program that includes aerobic activity, resistance training, agility drills, and stretching. This will help them perform better when playing the sport.

Exercises that focus on the heart and lungs are absolutely necessary for anyone looking to improve their pickleball endurance. Building your endurance and improving your overall fitness levels can be accomplished quite effectively through activities such as running, cycling, and swimming. Players should aim for 30–60 minutes of cardiovascular exercise, three–five times per week at the very least. In addition, high-intensity interval training, generally known as HIIT, is an excellent method for enhancing cardiovascular fitness and burning fat.

Pickleball players should also prioritize strength training because it can contribute to improvements in both their overall power and performance. The primary muscle groups in your body can benefit from resistance training activities like lunges, squats, and push-ups by increasing their strength and endurance. The goal of players should be to perform resistance training two to three times a week, with each session focused on a different muscle group. When doing resistance workouts, it is essential to ensure that you are utilizing the correct form and technique in order to avoid injury.

On the court, a player's speed and agility can be improved through the use of agility drills. Footwork and overall movement on the court can be improved by the use of a variety of drills, some of which include jumping drills, ladder drills, and cone drills. Players should strive to include two to three sessions of agility drills in their weekly program of strength training and conditioning. It is essential to begin with basic drills and then gradually move on to more complex drills as players improve their skills.

Because it helps increase flexibility and protects athletes from injury, stretching is an essential component of any program that aims to condition the body and build muscle. Pickleball players should stretch before and after each game, as well as on days when there are no matches scheduled. A player's total fitness program could benefit from including yoga and pilates, which are both good types of stretching and can be practiced anywhere. A great way to get warmed up before a game is to perform some dynamic stretches, like lunges with a twist and high knees, for example.

When it comes to pickleball, getting enough rest and recovering properly are equally as crucial as conditioning and strength training. Every night, players should make it a priority to obtain a sufficient amount of sleep, and they should schedule rest days as needed. In addition to being crucial for overall health, proper nutrition and hydration are also important for performance. It is essential to pay attention to indications from the body and refrain from overtraining in order to avoid injuries and maintain optimal performance.

Injury prevention and recovery

Players in the sport of pickleball are required to be quick and capable to change their direction at a moment's notice because the game moves at a fast pace and places a high demand on their physical fitness. Injury is a possibility in any activity; however, if players are aware of how to properly prevent injuries and recover from them, they may significantly lower their likelihood of getting hurt while still getting the most out of their time spent competing.

Injuries can cause players to miss games as well as practices, which can be damaging to both the individual player's development and the overall success of the team. Players are able to maintain their health and continue playing the sport they love as long as preventative measures are taken to reduce the risk of injury.

Accidents can result in significant losses, both in terms of time and money. It's easy for medical expenses, time lost from work, and physical therapy sessions to quickly pile up. In the long run, players and their families can save time and money if they take measures to reduce the risk of injury and take preventative measures.

Some injuries, such as chronic discomfort, joint difficulties, and decreased mobility, might have an influence on a player's health for a longer period of time than others. Players can lower their chances of having these problems later in life and continue playing pickleball for many years to come if they take steps to protect themselves against injury.

The importance of properly warming up before playing pickleball cannot be overstated. To get the blood flowing and the pulse rate up, players should begin with some modest cardiovascular exercise, such as jogging or jumping jacks. After this, you should do some dynamic stretching to get your muscles ready for the next exercise. Some examples of this include lunges with a twist and high knees.

When playing pickleball, it's important to make sure you have the right equipment ready. On the court, players should wear shoes that provide adequate support and have good traction to avoid slipping and falling. You can also use padded gloves to protect your hands from calluses and blisters.

The best way to avoid injuries when playing pickleball is to improve your technique through regular practice. When hitting the ball, players should pay attention to their footwork and form, as well as ensure that they are using the appropriate grip and swing technique. This can help avoid injuries caused by strain as well as those caused by overuse.

Pickleball players should prioritize rest and recovery in order to reduce their risk of injury. After participating in a game or practice, players should be sure to give their bodies time to heal by taking rest days when necessary. A sufficient amount of sleep and nutritious food are also essential for maintaining overall health and warding off injuries.

Injuries can keep players out of action for several weeks or even months, which can be extremely frustrating and difficult. Techniques for recovering from injuries that are done correctly can assist players in returning to the game sooner and reducing the amount of time they are out of action.

It's not uncommon for athletes to have the same injury over and over again, which may be extremely frustrating and discouraging for the player. Players might lessen their chances of suffering further injuries and maintain their health for subsequent matches if they properly recover from previous ones.

A person's emotional as well as their physical health might suffer as a result of an injury. Players can preserve their physical fitness and mental well-being by healing from injuries in the correct manner, which enables them to return to the game with the confidence and excitement they had before the injury.

In order to heal from an injury caused while playing pickleball, it is essential to rest and recover. Before getting back into the game, it's important for players to give their bodies some time to heal and recover. It's possible that this will need taking a break from the sport, doing some gentle exercise instead, and then gradually building up the intensity over time.

Pickleball players who have injuries may find that participating in physical therapy helps them recover more quickly. A physical therapist is able to devise an individualized treatment plan for their patients, which may consist of several types of exercises designed to help improve mobility, strength, and flexibility. In addition to this, they are able to offer guidance on the appropriate method and form to use in order to avoid further injuries.

The application of heat and ice to an injured area can be of assistance in relieving pain and inflammation, respectively. Ice can be applied to the affected area to assist reduce swelling and numb pain, while heat can help stimulate blood flow and promote healing in the area. Players should consult their primary care physician or a physical therapist to determine the most effective treatment plan for their specific injury.

During the healing process for an injury, it may be helpful to use pain management strategies, such as medicine or acupuncture, to help manage the pain. However, before beginning any new pain management routine, athletes should consult with their primary care physician to confirm the plan is both appropriate and successful for the player's particular injury.

Chapter VI

Advanced Techniques

Spin shots and specialty serves

The sports of tennis, badminton, and table tennis are all incorporated into pickleball, which is its own unique sport. Players use paddles to knock a lightweight ball back and forth across a net that is erected in the center of the court where the game is played. Pickleball is a game that requires both strategy and ability, and in order to participate at a high level, players need to have a wide variety of shots at their disposal. Players can get an advantage on the court by utilizing spin shots and specialty serves, which are two different types of shots.

When playing pickleball, the ability to create angles is one of the most significant advantages of spin shots. Players have the ability to make the ball bend in a variety of ways and produce surprising bounces by creating spin into the ball. Because of this, it is more difficult for the opponent to predict where the ball will land, which gives the player an edge. When hitting cross-court shots, spin shots can be particularly successful since the ball can curve away from the opponent and create an open court for the player to shoot into.

Changing the pace of the game can also be accomplished through the use of spin shots. Players can make it difficult for their opponents to get into a rhythm and react fast by giving the ball either topspin or backspin, which adds a spinning effect to the ball and can either speed up or slow down the ball. A player could, for instance, hit a high topspin shot to make the opponent to back up, and then immediately follow it up with a quick backspin shot to the lower court to catch the opponent off guard.

Spin shots may be a great way for players to bring variety and unpredictability to their games. Players can keep their opponents guessing and make it hard for them to anticipate what will coming next if they have a variety of different types of shots at their disposal. This may result in an increase in the number of opportunities to win points and acquire an edge while playing the game.

It takes practice to hit spin shots successfully. Players should spend time on the court practicing various kinds of spins and getting a feel for how the ball will behave in order to improve their game. In addition to this, it is essential to get plenty of experience hitting spin shots at a variety of speeds and angles. When it comes to any shot, a player's level of comfort and confidence will increase according to the amount of practice they put in.

Players should use their wrists as a means of adding spin onto the ball. Players can create spin and add curve to the ball by snapping their wrists at the point of contact with the ball. To generate the maximum spin possible, it is essential to have a loose wrist and to hold the paddle in a comfortable manner. Players should try out a variety of wrist angles to evaluate how these modifications affects the amount of spin that is imparted on the ball.

To keep their opponents guessing, players should change the spin that they put on their shots. They may produce a wide variety of shots by employing topspin, backspin, or sidespin in their shots. In order to add variety to their game, it is also essential to change the spin that they use on different shots. To throw off their opponent's equilibrium, a player might hit a forehand stroke with topspin, then immediately follow it up with a backhand shot with backspin.

Players have the potential to earn opportunities to win points by using specialty serves. Players can throw off their opponents and force them to make a mistake by using a creative serve, which can result in either a point for the player or an easier shot. You can also employ specialty serves to target a weakness in your opponent's game or take advantage of where they are positioned on the court.

In addition to this, specialty serves have the potential to throw off the rhythm of the opponent. Players can make it difficult for their opponents to anticipate what is going to occur next by using a unique serve, which forces their opponents to shift where they are positioned on the court in response. This may result in the server having an increased number of opportunities to win points and acquire an advantage on the court.

When a player incorporates specialty serves into their game, the result might be one that is more unpredictable and varied. Players are able to keep their opponents guessing and make it very difficult for them to anticipate what will come next if they have a variety of alternative serves at their disposal. This may result in an increase in the number of opportunities to win points and acquire an edge while playing the game.

It requires practice to hit specialty serves successfully. Players should spend time on the court practicing a variety of different sorts of serves and getting a feel for how the ball will react to their attempts. In addition, it is essential to get plenty of practice serving at a variety of speeds and angles. When it comes to any shot, a player's level of comfort and confidence will increase according to the amount of practice they put in.

Players should experiment with different kinds of serves so they can bring a greater variety to their games. They have a variety of spins, speeds, and positioning options at their disposal, which keeps their opponents guessing. Altering the serve at different moments in the game can create an element of surprise for the opponent and help them stay on their toes. As an illustration, a player might use a lob serve on one point and a drive serve on the next to throw off the opponent's rhythm and keep them off-balance.

When it comes to hitting specialty serves, confidence is absolutely necessary. The players should have confidence in their skills and rely on the preparation they have received. It is essential to keep one's attention on the serve and not worry about how the opponent will respond to it. Players have the opportunity to add an additional element of surprise to their game and maybe gain an advantage if they are self-assured in their ability to successfully return specialty serves.

A spin shot that produces a forward spin on the ball is referred to as a topspin shot. Because of the spin, the ball will drop swiftly and fall deep in the opponent's court, making it challenging for them to return it. Players are instructed to brush up on the ball and snap their wrists at the point of contact in order to hit topspin shots.

The backspin shot is a type of spin shot that causes the ball to spin in the opposite direction of what was intended. Because of this spin, the ball will float and bounce low, making it impossible for the opponent to return the ball with any kind of force. Backspin is created when players brush down on the ball and utilize a relaxed grip. Hitting a backspin stroke requires players to execute both of these things.

The sidespin shot is a type of spin shot that rotates the ball to the left or right instead of forward and backward. This spin causes the ball to curve in the air as it travels and causes it to drop at an unexpected angle. This makes it difficult for opponents to predict where the ball will land, which makes it more difficult for them to win. Players need to make contact with the ball on the edge of the paddle and then quickly snap their wrist in the desired direction to execute a sidespin shot.

The drop shot is a specialized form of serving that entails making a light contact with the ball and then dropping it just beyond the net. This shot has the potential to take opponents by surprise and cause them to race to the net in order to get the ball back. Players need to have a light touch and a relaxed grip in order to successfully hit a drop shot. This allows them to lightly tap the ball over the net.

The lob serve is a specialized type of serve that involves striking the ball extremely high and deep into the court of the opponent. This serve has the potential to make opponents to take a step back, giving the player who is serving an advantage in the rally. Players need to smash the ball in a high arc and direct it toward the back of the court in order to successfully execute a lob serve.

The drive serve is a specialized type of serve that consists of hitting the ball with a lot of force and speed toward the court of the opponent. This serve has the potential to surprise the opponent, which will put pressure on them to respond swiftly in order to return the ball. Players should utilize a hard swing and aim for the opponent's weaker side in order to successfully hit a drive serve.

The Ernie shot is a specialized shots that requires the player to run around the non-volley zone in order to strike a ball that is approaching the player's backhand. This shot has the potential to take opponents by surprise and force them to cover more ground in a shorter amount of time. Players need to have quick reflexes and the ability to strike the ball with power and accuracy from a difficult angle in order to be successful at hitting an Ernie shot.

The fake serve is a form of specialty serve that consists of pretending to serve and then hitting a different kind of serve after the opponent has returned the serve. This might throw off an opponent's game plan and force them to make a quick response to the new serve. Players should go through the motions of their regular serve, but at the very last second, they should draw back and hit a different style of serve. This is how players can successfully execute a fake serve.

A specialty serve known as the half-serve is performed by striking the ball in a manner that is halfway between a lob serve and a drive serve. This serve has the potential to take opponents by surprise and push them to make adjustments to their position on the court. Players should hit the ball at a medium speed and aim for the center of the opponent's court when attempting to hit a half-serve.

Advanced footwork and positioning

Pickleball is a sport that needs quick reactions, precise shots, as well as excellent footwork and positioning. It is a sport that moves quickly and is very dynamic. Players need to be able to move fast and effectively around the court, anticipate the shots that their opponents are going to take, and position themselves strategically so that they can maintain control of the game in order to compete at a high level.

It is essential for players to have advanced footwork and positioning since these skills enable them to move around the court more swiftly and effectively. Players are able to predict the shots that their opponents are going to take and move quickly to intercept them if they have good footwork and are in the appropriate position. The players' chances of succeeding in the rally and gaining points are improved as a result of this potential advantage.

Shot selection can also be improved by footwork and positioning that are more advanced. Players have the ability to make better educated selections regarding which shots to make and where to hit them if they are in the appropriate position on the court. This can lead to a more strategic and effective shot selection, which in turn can result in a higher level of play as well as an increase in the number of successful points.

A reduction in fatigue is another benefit of having good footwork and positioning. Players are able to save energy and prevent unnecessary movements that may tire them out if they move properly and ensure that they are in the optimal position at all times.

This can help them build their endurance, which in turn will enable them to play at a high level for extended periods of time.

Keep your feet moving at all times. This is one of the most crucial pieces of advice for advanced footwork in pickleball. This requires you to continuously shift your position on the court and be prepared to make quick movements in any given direction. You can maintain your balance and be in a better position to respond to the shots that your opponent takes if you keep your feet moving.

Keep your weight distributed evenly across both balls of your feet as you take your footwork to the next level. Because of this, you will be able to move around the court quickly and efficiently, as well as be prepared to respond to the shots taken by your opponent. Keeping your equilibrium and avoiding being taken off guard are both made easier as a result of this.

The split-step is an essential footwork technique in pickleball that entails springing up and landing with your feet shoulder-width apart as your opponent smashes the ball. This enables you to instantly reverse course and travel in the direction of the ball so that you can intercept it. You can boost your response speed and your chances of making successful shots if you use the split-step technique.

One further key part of excellent footwork and positioning in pickleball is the ability to anticipate the shots that your opponent will be making. You will be able to predict your opponent's shots and position yourself appropriately if you pay attention to their game and pay attention to the patterns of their shots. You will have a better chance of winning points and the rally if you do this, as it will give you an advantage.

The non-volley zone, which is often referred to as the kitchen, is an essential region of the court that calls for strategic footwork and positioning. You may exert more influence over the pace of the match and push your opponent to take more difficult shots if you are in the appropriate position in the non-volley zone. It is important that you are aware of the rules pertaining to the non-volley zone and that you utilize it to your benefit.

How to deal with difficult shots

Pickleball is a sport that involves quick reactions, precise shooting, and the ability to think strategically. On the other hand, even the top players often have trouble dealing with difficult shots that are hard to return or put back into play. Players need to be able to handle a wide variety of shots and adapt to a number of playing styles in order to be successful at the sport of pickleball.

A shot known as the lob is one that is hit very high into the air, typically going over the head of the opponent. This shot can be difficult to return since the player must swiftly move to the back of the court and hit the ball while it is still in the air. This makes it a challenging shot for both offense and defense. Players have the option of using the lob as a tactic to force their opponents into retreating and open up space for themselves to make a winning shot.

The drop shot is a type of shot in which the ball gets hit gently and settles just over the net. This shot can be challenging to return since the player must rapidly rush to the front of the court and hit the ball before it bounces twice. This requires the player to move quickly. The drop shot is a technique that can be utilized to throw off the opponents' game plan and forcing them to race to the net in order to get the ball.

A shot is considered to be made with a spin when it is hit with either topspin, backspin, or sidespin. Due to the fact that it can change direction or bounce in an unpredictable manner, this shot can be challenging to return. The spin shot provides an opportunity to generate spaces and angles on the court as well as to throw off the rhythm of the opponent.

The Ernie shot is a type of stroke that requires the player to go around the non-volley zone in order to hit a ball that is approaching the player's backhand. This shot can be challenging to return since the player must smash the ball with power and accuracy while coming at it from an awkward angle. It is possible to throw off your opponents with an Ernie shot, which will require them to cover more ground in a short amount of time.

The first piece of advice for overcoming challenging shots in pickleball is to keep your concentration. It is critical to maintain focus on the ball at all times and try to guess where it will travel next. Maintaining your concentration will allow you to be more prepared to move quickly and take an accurate shot.

When attempting tough shots in pickleball, having solid footwork is absolutely necessary. You can place yourself in the best position to make a shot, and increase your chances of doing so, by moving around the court in a quick and efficient manner. It is essential to keep your feet moving at all times and to employ the split-step technique in order to quickly change directions.

Practicing your response to challenging shots is one of the most effective methods to improve your ability to handle them in the future. You can gain the necessary abilities and strategies to make good returns if you practice making a variety of shots with a partner or a coach and work together to improve your game.

Dealing with difficult shots involves a number of significant aspects, one of which is anticipating the shots of your opponent. You will be able to predict your opponent's shots and position yourself appropriately if you pay attention to their game and pay attention to the patterns of their shots. This can offer you an advantage during the rally, and it can also improve the likelihood that your returns will be successful.

Being creative is oftentimes the most effective approach to taking care of challenging shots. To accomplish this, you might try a different kind of shot, strike the ball from a different angle, or move in an unexpected way. You can take your opponent by surprise and earn a potential advantage in the rally if you are creative and think outside the box.

Chapter VII

Resources and Community

Where to find pickleball courts and clubs

Pickleball is a sport that is becoming increasingly popular and is played by people of varying ages and levels of expertise. The game is played on a court that is about the same size as a court used for badminton, and it may be played in either an indoor or outdoor setting.

Courts for the sport of pickleball can frequently be found in public parks and other types of recreational centers. Due to the increasing number of people interested in playing pickleball, many parks and recreation departments have decided to incorporate specialized pickleball courts into their existing facilities. Courts like these are frequently available to the general public and can be rented for use. Players can check the website of their community's parks and recreation department or give the office a call to inquire about the availability of pickleball courts.

Courts for pickleball can typically be found in a variety of locations, including the YMCA and community centers. Pickleball leagues and classes are frequently provided by these facilities for players of varying skill levels. They might also offer pickleball courts that are available to members as well as people who are not members of the club. Players should contact their neighborhood YMCA or community center to inquire about the availability of pickleball programs and to learn the hours during which courts can be used for games.

Due to the growing popularity of pickleball, a number of educational institutions, including universities, have built specific courts for the sport within their athletic facilities. There is a possibility that members of the general public will be able to utilize these courts, particularly during the months of summer when schools are not in session. Players should inquire with the local schools and institutions in their area to determine whether or not pickleball courts are available for usage and to find out the hours during which they are open for play.

There are also a great number of private clubs and facilities that make their members' use of pickleball courts available to them. There is a possibility that these clubs provide players of varying skill levels with leagues, tournaments, and clinics. Court use by individuals who are not members of the facility may be possible at some privately owned facilities for a fee. Players can inquire with the country clubs, fitness clubs, and other private facilities in their immediate area to determine whether or not they provide pickleball programs and to learn the hours during which the courts are open for play.

Players can also identify pickleball courts and groups in their region by consulting one of the many internet tools that are currently accessible. Directory information about pickleball clubs and venues may be found on a variety of websites, including USAPA.org and PickleballTournaments.com, amongst others. Players can also utilize social media sites such as Facebook and Meetup to interact with other players in their region and learn about local clubs and leagues. These platforms are designed specifically for this purpose.

Researching the area in which you want to play pickleball is one of the most important piece of advice that can be given. Players can consult internet resources and get in touch with the parks and recreation agencies, schools, and universities in their communities, as well as private clubs, to learn where pickleball courts are located and what time they are open for play.

Joining local pickleball groups on social media platforms such as Facebook and Meetup can be an excellent way to interact with other players in your area and learn about local pickleball clubs and leagues. These associations could also be able to provide information about newly constructed pickleball courts and other facilities in your area.

Participating in pickleball activities such as tournaments, clinics, and exhibitions can be an excellent opportunity to meet new people who play the sport as well as get additional knowledge about it. It's possible that these events will also provide information on local leagues and clubs that are available in your area.

How to get involved in the pickleball community

Pickleball is a sport that is loved by individuals of all ages and ability levels. It is a sport that is both enjoyable and exciting. It is an excellent way to stay active, meet new people, and become a part of a community that is thriving and expanding at the same time.

Joining a local pickleball club or league is one of the most effective methods to get more active in the pickleball community. Pickleball clubs and leagues can be found in many different places, and they often provide their members with opportunities to participate in regular matches, tournaments, and social gatherings. Participating in a club or league is an excellent opportunity to make new friends, pick up useful skills, and maintain an active lifestyle. Players can do a search online for local clubs and leagues in their region, or they can check with their community's parks and recreation department, to learn about possibilities to participate in a game of their choice.

Participating in pickleball competitions and other activities is another fantastic opportunity to become engaged in the local community. Watching some of the finest players in the sport compete against one another, learning new skills, and meeting other players from throughout the country are all fantastic reasons to participate in tournaments. Players have the opportunity to connect with others who share their enthusiasm for the sport while also improving their skill at the numerous clinics and other events that are offered in conjunction with many tournaments.

A fantastic way to become involved in the community and give back to the sport of pickleball is to offer your services as a volunteer at one of its tournaments. The success of many competitions and events is based on the participation of volunteers who can assist with activities such as scorekeeping, court setup, and registration. Volunteering is a fantastic way to connect with other players, increase one's knowledge of the game, and make a positive contribution to one's community.

Connecting with other pickleball players and becoming active in the pickleball community can be facilitated through the use of online forums and social media platforms. A significant number of players make use of online communities and forums, such as Facebook, Meetup, and Reddit, to network with other players in their region, discuss helpful hints and methods, and keep updated of the most recent developments in the sport. Participating in pickleball-oriented online forums can be an excellent way to network with other players and cultivate meaningful connections with people who share your passion for the sport.

Participating in pickleball clinics and workshops is yet another fantastic way to become engaged in the pickleball community and enhance your skills on the court. Numerous organizations, including leagues and clubs, host clinics and workshops on various aspects of the game, including strategies, footwork, and technique. Participating in these events is a fantastic way to enhance your game, as well as acquire new skills and network with other players.

Conclusion

Recap of key points

An e-book with the title "Pickleball for Beginners: A Step-by-Step Guide to Learning and Playing Pickleball" has been written with the intention of assisting new players in learning the fundamentals of the sport and getting started with playing pickleball. In the following paragraphs, we will review some of the most essential topics that were discussed in the e-book, as well as highlight some of the most crucial recommendations and strategies that are aimed toward novice players who are attempting to improve their game.

The Basics of Pickleball

The fundamentals of pickleball, including as the court dimensions, the required equipment, and the rules of the game, are covered in the beginning chapter of the e-book. In addition to this, it discusses the many strokes that players have at their disposal, including as the serve, the forehand, the backhand, and the dink.

How to Choose the Right Equipment

Pickleball is a sport that requires careful preparation, including the selection of appropriate gear. The e-book discusses not only the various kinds of paddles and balls that can be purchased, but also the various aspects that players need to take into consideration when selecting their equipment, such as the paddle's weight, the size of the grip, and the material.

Essential Techniques for Playing Pickleball

The e-book offers detailed instructions on how to perform some of the fundamental skills necessary to play pickleball, such as the correct grip, footwork, and body positioning. In addition to this, it provides guidance on how to avoid making some of those common mistakes that are made by beginners.

Strategies and Tactics for Winning the Game

Pickleball is a sport that needs players to use strategy and technique in order to come out on top. The e-book discusses some of the most important strategies and techniques that players may implement to improve their game. These include playing to their opponent's weaknesses, moving their opponent around the court, and utilizing a variety of shots to keep their opponent off-balance.

Tips for Staying Safe and Injury-Free

It's crucial to remember to take precautions when playing pickleball so you don't hurt yourself. This e-book goes over some of the most important safety recommendations that players should always keep in mind. Some of these include warming up before playing, maintaining proper hydration, and wearing footwear that is suitable for the activity.

How to Improve Your Game

Players who are looking to enhance their game and take their skills to the next level can take advantage of the tips and tactics that are provided in the e-book. These pointers include making consistent practice a part of your routine, playing against opponents of varying skill levels, and concentrating on the aspects of your play that could use some work.

Final thoughts and encouragement to keep playing

Pickleball is a sport that is played by millions of people all over the world because it is both entertaining and thrilling. It is an excellent way to stay active, meet new people, and become a part of a community that is thriving and expanding at the same time.

Pickleball is a sport that can be enjoyed by individuals of all ages and ability levels, which is one of the many reasons why it is considered to be such a wonderful activity. On the court, there is always more to learn, regardless of whether you are a novice or an experienced player, and there are always new challenges to take on. Pickleball is a sport that is simple to pick up but challenging to perfect, making it an excellent option for players who are searching for a game that will both provide them with enjoyment and a sense of accomplishment.

Pickleball, like any other activity or hobby, demands dedication and time investment on your part. It is essential for players to prioritize pickleball in their lives and find a way to fit the sport into their hectic schedules so that they can participate. Players ought to make an intentional effort to maintain pickleball a regular part of their routine, and this effort could take the form of signing up for a local club or league, going to tournaments and events, or simply finding the time to play with their friends.

The community of pickleball players is one of the sport's most appealing aspects, and it's also one of its greatest strengths. Players have the opportunity to improve their game, acquire new abilities, and form new friendships when they interact with other pickleball players and become active members of the pickleball community. Players should make an effort to be a part of the pickleball community and create relationships with other players, and this may be done in a variety of ways, including joining a local club or league, participating in tournaments and events, or communicating with other players online.

The sport of pickleball necessitates ongoing education and development in order to be played at a high level. Even the most seasoned athletes can always find new methods to hone their skills and improve their performance on the court. Players should always be looking for methods to enhance their game and take their talents to the next level, and this could involve attending clinics and seminars, practicing on a consistent basis, or even competing against other players who have varying degrees of experience.

Pickleball is a sport that should, first and foremost, be played in a cheerful and joyful manner. It is essential to keep in mind the excitement and enjoyment of the game at all times, regardless of whether you are participating in a highly competitive competition or simply hitting the ball around with friends. Players must keep their attention on having a good time on the court rather than being overly preoccupied with whether they are winning or losing. Players have the potential of continuing to love and respect the sport for many years to come if the emphasis remains on having fun and taking pleasure in it.

In conclusion, pickleball is a wonderful sport which offers players of all ages and ability levels with a wide range of benefits that may be enjoyed. Players are able to continue reaping the benefits of playing pickleball as long as they devote sufficient time and energy to the sport, maintain meaningful relationships with other enthusiasts, and strive for continuous growth and development. On the court, there is always more to learn, regardless of whether you are a novice or an experienced player, and there are always new challenges to take on. Pickleball is a beautiful sport, so keep on participating in it, keep on having fun with it, and keep on appreciating all of the thrills and challenges that it has to offer.

Thank you for buying and reading/listening to our book. If you found this book useful/helpful please take a few minutes and leave a review on Amazon.com or Audible.com (if you bought the audio version).